Bromley's Hurricane

MURIEL V. SEARLE

KENTISH TIMES NEWSPAPERS

ACKNOWLEDGEMENTS

THE author wishes most sincerely to thank the many people who helped in the compilation of this book, especially by loaning pictures. In particular: Jill Baldwin; Avryl Bavister; C T Bird; Paul Bowen; Nicholas Bradley; Bristol Street Motors; British Rail; Bromley Central Library, Local Studies; Bromley Football Club; Bromley Ladies' & Men's Barber Shop Harmony Clubs; Andrew Burgess; S R Clark; Dolcis Shoe Shop; ENBRO(Environment Bromley) and Philip Daniell; Chris Evans; Rita Evans; Beth Fender; Tracy Gayton; Coral Gibson; Brian Glassborow; Mrs A Gurley; Hayes Afternoon TWG: Hayes Library; John Hayhow; High Elms Nature Centre; Lesley Hirst; Bridget Hollman; Mike Lewis; London Borough of Bromley (various departments at Civic Centre); Clr. P Mansfield; Tom Martin; Alan Miles; Councillor Albert Miles; Jean Morgan; Owen Photographic; A J Packham Anne Paterson; Polhill Garden Centre Ltd and Mrs R S Novell; Rev J Poole; Princes Plain School; John Puttock; Rev D Redman; Mrs J Richmond & Emma; RSPCA; Seismograph Service Ltd; Southborough Primary School; Roger Spencer; Mr & Mrs C Williams and Newstead Wood School; Margaret Voisey; Gordon Winn; John Topham; Woodrose Furniture Co Ltd and Bob Goodsir. In preparing such a topical book at speed, it would be easy unwittingly to omit a name; should this have happened, it is hoped that sincerest appreciation will be accepted.

ISBN 0 9513464 0 7

Published by Kentish Times Newspapers,
44 Harmer Street,
Gravesend,
Kent DA12 2AY.

Printed in Great Britain by Staples Printers (Rochester) Ltd,
Love Lane,
Rochester.

FOREWORD
Mayor's Parlour 25th April 1988

BY the time Bromley's Book of the Hurricane is published, I shall no longer be Mayor, but the events of the night of 15th/16th October 1987 are firmly imprinted in my mind as THE unplanned event of my year of office.

As former Mayor, therefore, and Patron of the 1000 Tree Appeal so successfully run by the Kentish Times and Bromley Council, I am honoured to have been asked to write this foreword and delighted that Muriel Searle and the Kentish Times have responded to a wish I have heard expressed many times over: namely that "someone should write a book about it."

Once in 150 years or so, I am told, there may come such a storm as we recently lived through. This book is therefore a very personal record for Bromley people, not only as a reminder of the devastation which was so swiftly cleared away but, in addition, as a historical record for our children and grandchildren.

All of you who so generously supported the 1000 Tree Appeal and the many thousands who came to the Trees for Tomorrow exhibition at the Civic Centre will, I am sure, welcome this publication as warmly as I do.

Councillor John Lewis - Mayor 1987 - 1988

INTRODUCTION

EVERY area of England has its own individual recorded history, whose landmark events are quite separate from those of national history: the Great Fire of Northampton; the Silvertown explosion; the sinking of the Mary Rose at Portsmouth; the Monmouth Rebellion in Somerset. But one particular date is common to almost everywhere from Oxford to Orpington, Minehead to Margate: 26 November 1703, the night known to posterity simply as The Great Storm. All other storms since have been measured against it but have never equalled it, and its savagery remained legendary for nearly three centuries. In a full week of violent weather culminating in that extraordinary night, about eight thousand people died, nationwide, ranging from a bishop killed in his bedroom as part of his palace collapsed, to a man-of-war lost off Kent with 386 hands.

Kent fared cruelly in 1703, at sea and ashore. Near home, surviving records portray the entire spire of Hayes church snapping completely off and being hurled across the churchyard into fragments, complete with bell. The rest of the building, according to the Vicar of St Mary Cray with Orpington, "received great damage". The destruction cost the parish dearly by early 18th century standards, including sixpence (2½p) paid to the man engaged to clear the heaps of wreckage from the churchyard.

The decline of St Mary Cray as a small market town was attributed to the destruction in the storm of its vital market hall. However, there were also remarkable escapes, as when a long stable block at St Mary Cray was lifted bodily off its foundations, and flung into the road in a heap of rubble, leaving five horses and one man standing unhurt in their places together with an intact manger of hay, "to the admiration of all beholders".

Nearby, a poor family left their beds only moments before their roof caved in, though a less quick moving clergyman of South-Ash hesitated almost fatally, getting out of bed in time to save his life but not his foot. "The effects of the hurricane and tempest of wind, rain and lightning" laid waste the country estate of the diarist Evelyn who, living at Deptford, was a regular traveller through Bromley (and once was mugged on Bromley Common).

Thankfully, however, the Great Storm of 1703 was as unique as the Great Fire of London in 1666, unlikely ever to be repeated.

In modern England hurricanes simply do not happen. At least, not until the night (or, rather, very early morning) of 16 October 1987, when the storm named "Hurricane Len" roared in from nowhere, unheralded by alarming forecasts, and devasted Bromley borough on a scale not seen for 284 years.

Its sheer unexpectedness was perhaps its most frightening aspect. Probably 99% of the citizens who went to bed on 15 October had never heard of the Great Storm, known only to historians. Few had studied their barometers around midnight; just as well for their peace of mind.

Some newspapers actually referred to the lowest readings ever observed in England; but were their reporters aware of 1703, or merely dramatising their stories?

Fortunately the painstaking Daniel Defoe not only recorded the Great Storm in minute detail; he even tracked the barometer's performance through the approaching hours, enabling us to check against an actual figure.

Even more fortunately, he chose figures for Upminster in Essex, only about twenty miles from Bromley as the hurricane-buffeted crow flies, where at the climax of 12.30 midnight on 26 November 1703, the reading was 972mb. (28.72 inches).

A call to the Meteorological Office quickly produced a reading for 16 October 1987 for a point about the same distance away, Gravesend. At 3am the reading there was an unprecedented 963mb (about 28.44 inches): lower, indeed, than for the Great Storm. No wonder Bromley looked like a battlefield, its hundreds of lovely trees blown, beaten, sucked, twisted and blasted from the ground. That structural damage was not so comparable must be attributed to the nature of modern building, compared with the predominating timber and thatch of the 18th century.

The author had better reason than most Bromleians to have noticed any ominous note to the previous night's weather forecast, being due to sail on the 16th to America aboard the QE2; any mention of severe gales would have been more consciously noted than normally. But, like eveyone else in the Borough, she went unsuspectingly to bed.

Three hours later the house was suddenly a giant punch-bag, thumped until the walls shuddered. Screeching winds tore at the lamp standard outside; the glowing orange light jumped and jitterbugged too fast for the eye to assimilate, a strange sight until it went out, along with the rest of the street. So did every light in Bromley - and every light in the whole of London.

Above the roaring darkness an all-night BBC announcer, working by emergency generator and heard over a battery operated radio, described with tangible awe his view of the whole of London as nobody had seen it since the Blitz: not a street light, or a house light, or a traffic light; just a vast blackness huddled under what we all now realised must be a hurricane.

And out there, already, were men called out in indescribable conditions and total darkness to begin working on fallen cables and blocked roads to restore the world to rights, though the sheer magnitude of their task could not be apparent until daylight.

Who will forget the dawning of 16 October? Or who, coming after us, will fully believe it? The wind still raged so high that even opening the front door was almost impossible, dragged inwards by natural suction. Huge trees sprawled everywhere . No trains, no buses, no light, no heat, no hot water, no telephone, no traffic lights; and precious little traffic until a briefly resurrected "Battle of Britain spirit" turned individual householders into teams, sawing and hacking at the nearest wreckage instead of waiting for the Council to arrive, opening narrow gaps for cars to crawl round. A few yards forward, and they joined another queue to push through tangled branches, or force an impromptu new road onto a verge and around another fallen giant. Out of the town itself, drivers felt disorientated after half an hour of this tree slalom course, so changed was every yard of the way with every familiar feature either destroyed or hidden behind barriers of leaves. Even now, more than six months later, country ramblers experience the same effect, convinced they have never been down a particular path before because it is so totally changed as to be unrecognisable.

Initial estimates suggested that, though the Great Storm outdid Hurricane Len in human carnage, Len surpassed 1703 in natural destruction. Throughout Kent in 1703 about 17,000 trees collapsed; in 1987 the figure was about 15,000 for Bromley alone - and that only for trees along highways and streets; the number fallen in the countryside and commons would be difficult to calculate. They ranged from a familiar urban corner denuded of three out of five trees, to an entire wood wiped out, as at High Elms. One rough estimate put the loss at perhaps sixty thousand.

Though many witnesses described crashing trunks adding to the general uproar, countryside wardens believe that some actually "floated down" with no cataclysmic crash, simply leaning lower and lower as successive groups of roots parted with each buffet of winds gusting at anything up to 100mph. By the time the last roots went, the tree was already near the ground. Once fallen, its exposed roots are believed to have dried out in as little as two hours after the rain ceased; the tree would have been dead soon after dawn.

There were, of course, the individual tragedies; above all, the almost total destruction of Beechy Walk at High Elms; that long narrow avenue running from top to bottom of a hill in perfect geometrical symmetry, where horses ambled up through sunlight and shadow of the closely spaced trunks. Now, only a few remain at the top; since clearance, the rest of the hillside is a vast, bleak and gaunt emptiness, bare as yet even of one blade of grass.

Nature was also ironical. Inside the dead trunk of ancient Wilberforce Oak at Keston, a younger oak had been growing for about a generation. But it was the sturdy-looking youngster that crashed, leaving the battered old hulk standing. More ironically, the historic stone Wilberforce Seat, moved recently to protect it from vandalism, took the brunt of the fallen wreckage, which missed its original site - fortunately, without notable damage. We have discovered several old trees at Chislehurst marked for felling before the storm, standing defiantly upright with supposedly sound neighbours at their feet.

At Hayes a small orchard stood untouched, but each tree had a neat circular footbath of fallen ripe apples, their entire crop shaken off at once.

Two of the commonest stories were of the gleeful householder who found some massive but protected tree he had vainly pleaded to be allowed to fell, lying flat next day. And the one who found a similar tree the only one left standing. And, of course, scores of lucky residents found trees that had missed them by feet or even by inches, having obligingly fallen the other way. Scores of others, though, experienced the devastation of trees falling directly through their roofs and gables.

Every area had its own visible proof of the sheer power of the invisible wind. In the Market Square it was a tangle of scaffolding and timber wrenched off a bank, filling much of the roadway between it and Allders store; in daylight, how many shoppers must have been there? In the Civic Centre, it was historic trees under which Bishops of Rochester had strolled while thinking out their sermons, or Lords of the Manor taking the air by the Palace lake. On Martin's Hill it was the familiar evergreens; enough holly berries to decorate half Bromley lay there, but too early for Christmas; and the High Street seasonal decorations, completed only one day before, were wrapped round the lamp posts; hours of dedicated work must have lain behind the achievement of still lighting them as planned, albeit with missing parts to many of the setpieces.

At Shortlands, casualties included a fig tree rescued when the stationmaster's house was demolished for the present car park, dating from a time when Shortlands was the station for Bromley. It had been successfully transplanted to the garden outside

St Mary's church in the belief that it would be safe: until Hurricane Len knocked it flat. It is hoped that the remains, pruned hard back, will recover enough to keep a fragment of local railway history alive.

Hayes suffered severely, not only on the commons where many birches were felled, but nearer the centre. Devastated Husseywell Gardens remained closed for several weeks, used partly as a trees' crematorium; as elsewhere in Bromley, the scent of burning timber and the sound of chain saws were the dominant memories of late 1987. Across the road a gigantic cedar, perhaps three hundred years old, sprawled outside Hayes Library. With the equally giant beech lying by the steps in High Broom Wood it was among the most spectacular casualties in terms of size. Again one asked: how could unseen wind, without tangible substance, knock down a trunk which normally might need two or three harnessed bulldozers? Some measure of this wind's force was brought home to the author in America. Wherever she travelled during the following three weeks, virtually every American had the same question for a visiting Englishwoman: what was it like in the hurricane? And Americans are accustomed to hurricanes, and also to assuming that European disasters are small and unnewsworthy compared with their own.

Small landscape features were newly created, to further change the familiar world, like the large mounds of wood chippings in Jubilee Country Park. Nobody had seen such quantities before.

Luckily, few historic structures were badly damaged apart from the ancient lychgate at St John the Baptist at West Wickham; not because a tree toppled onto it, but because the roots, spreading unseen beneath the gate, pulled up one of the side supports as they were dragged out of the earth. The rest collapsed into the resulting hole. The remains were carefully set aside in a neat pile, with the main roof framework, pending restoration. More noticeable from a distance was the general bareness of the scene. The church stood bleakly on its hill, its picturesqueness temporarily reduced. Across the whole south-east of England it was estimated that about fifteen million trees died that night; and even fifteen make a startling difference to a landscape where nature and an historic building have for centuries complemented each other.

Farnborough lost three irreplaceable beauties; not only Beechy Walk and its surrounding woods, but also Old Hill and Church Road. A year ago, both the latter were sunken tunnels of leaves almost meeting overhead, embanked with thick vegetation. Today, they look as if a motorway were being driven through with harsh chalky banks as bare as concrete, and as yet devoid even of a grass covering. The trunks above them are gone, and in parts of the long belt of trees parallel to Church road more were left lying prone than standing up, instead of sheltering the historic Lubbock family graves and a large badger colony. No site better sums up October 16, 1987, than Church Road. Many motorists describe becoming disorientated on entering it for the first time since the hurricane, so unrecognisable was a once over familiar road. Similarly, even countryside wardens for some time made the same admission at Petts Wood, constantly finding themselves without bearings on paths they thought they knew blindfold; they all looked alike without their individual landmarks, be it one small but recognisable bush, or a complete group of oaks.

Interestingly, history itself became reversed on Chislehurst Common, as well as geography. The woods we assumed were ancient dated in fact mainly from the present century; pictures from before 1900 show Chislehurst to be much more open, spacious enough to include a racecourse and to accomodate the 100,000 sightseers at the Prince Imperial's funeral with a clear view. On Prince Imperial walk, so many trees fell as to restore something of this old appearance, when a common was grassy grazing land, common to local people and their livestock, rather than the thickly wooded scene that Chislehurst became.

Of course, there was also a bright side: there always is. At least four bright sides: the unwitting comedy; ordinary peoples' heroism; the fortunate escapes; and nature's eventual compensation.

In the first category came the owner of a certain large secluded garden. Next morning most of his trees were intact. So was the shed sitting in the middle of his lawn - except that it had not been there when he went to bed. Unless it unlatched the gate, walked in and closed the gate behind it, the only inference is that the shed flew over the tall hedges to land upright and undamaged in a convenient place. Weeks of enquiry failed ever to establish where it came from.

Or there was Bromley's politest tree, which obligingly fell outwards through an open garden gate, across the road, and into another open gate on the other side, scarcely damaging either.

Or the high heeled shoe that ran, with no foot inside it, from a damaged shop at Elmfield Road halfway to Bromley South, as if catching a train.

Not to mention the victim-who-never-was; a woman walking her dog next morning who supposedly trod on a still live power cable snapped off the pylons crossing Biggin Hill, killing them both; exhaustive enquiries by a reporter hoping for a good story, from the police, fire brigade, and local hospitals, draw a complete blank, illustrating the inventive power of gossip that always tries to decorate an already dramatic event.

There was the prone birch which, when one limb was sawed off, immediately sprang perfectly upright again, with the slightly obscene sound of a giant bow and arrow. And the mingled humour and public-spiritedness prompting a garage to turn an extremely squashed car, complete with embedded trunk, into a temporary "hurricane sculpture", surrounded by both wreckage and new young saplings, as topical publicity for a replacement tree appeal.

We all know of unsung local heroes. Men called out long before dawn while the storm still raged, working in the worst winds for 284 years to start repairing fallen cables and restore power; the first lights began appearing by mid-morning.

The owner of a Keston cattery who, though pregnant, went out alone by lanternlight at two in the morning to transfer the most frightened of her boarders to indoor houses.

The neighbour who drove the author through a five-hour obstacle course to check the safety of one cat there, and then all the way back through innumerable road blockages, and on to London, saving an American holiday that would undoubtedly have been lost.

The Biggin Hill crews who, with damaged aircraft all around, got photographers and officials into the air to assess the situation more clearly and to film this unique event for posterity. This video raised great interest at the eventual hurricane exhibition at the Civic Centre, and was also made available to the public as a lasting souvenir.

Escapes there were plenty. Representative of the many, might be cited the taxi driver pinned down not by one tree but by two, falling within seconds of each other as he drove, and who lived to tell this tall-sounding but true tale. Many a family escaped because a tree fell on an unoccupied bedroom, or was stopped by one corner of a roof, or a shed in the right place.

Nature's compensation emerged as early as January 1988, when she sent an unusually mild uneventful winter (after three savage seasons in a row), as if ensuring that the birds, animals and insects whose habitat was destroyed would stand the best chance.

By March the lost tree beauty overhead was compensated underfoot by wild flowers taking over, cashing in on extra light and less competition for nourishment; great swathes of white violets, as well as the commoner mauve, appeared at High Elms where previously one had noticed only a handful. Carpets of bluebells were covering ground left barren after tree losses, promising the best displays for years.

The bared banks where Beechy Walk used to be, were expected to become rich in four varieties of wild summer orchids, facing south into open sunlight. Countryside wardens here were confident by February that 1988 would be a bumper year for wild flowers of all kinds.

Nevertheless, the fact remained that Bromley had lost much of its greatest asset: the trees justifying its recent slogan of "Clean and green".

One oak at Chislehurst that was old when the Napoleons walked under it at Camden leaves only its own empty gap. When large numbers fall at once in such a location, the entire landscape changes for good. An organised plan was obviously needed if people a century ahead were to see the borough as we did before October 1987; for no oak or beech sapling planted now will mature in any of our present lifetimes. The old saying that planting a tree one will never see fully grown is an act of faith, was never more true.

In such faith was born the Thousand Tree Appeal; and in such faith it swelled beyond its original aim of raising the cost of a thousand young trees for beautifying some of the worst devastated spots. Jointly the *Kentish Times* and the London Borough of Bromley invited the public to specify where in the Borough they each wanted their money to be used, the average cost of a seven-year-old sapling being £10. Shortly before Christmas the target stood a mere £26.46 short; until a cheque for just over that sum came in from a Beckenham school. "You did it!" *the Times* congratulated Bromleians, with 450 trees already planted — and suggested making it a Two Thousand Tree Appeal. When it finally closed in the following spring, the total raised was £27,397.

Hurricane Len was undoubtedly the most ferocious wind storm touching England since Defoe described "the greatest and the longest storm that ever the world saw" nearly three centuries ago. Frightening though it was at the time, and devasting its damage, we can at least say to our children's children that we lived through a truly unique experience.

Muriel V. Searle
April 1988.

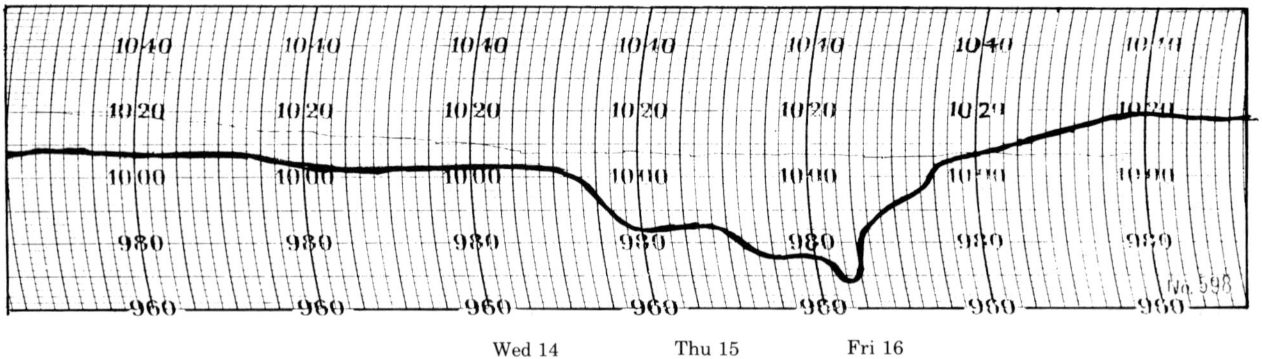

Barograph from the weather station at Nelson Close, Biggin Hill, showing the strength of the hurricane (highlighted line).

The scene which said all that need be said about what might have been. In daylight, how many cars, buses and other vehicles would have been in Bromley Market Square on an average day, and how many shoppers on the pavement, when this avalanche of scaffolding slid off Barclays Bank?

A road sign in Market Square was left telling a blatant lie. Chislehurst, Lee Green and Grove Park all appeared to be straight down in the direction of Australia, while other traffic was directed straight through Allders' front door!

This entire frontage of a Bromley High Street shoe store, only recently completely redesigned, was blown out. Glass piled so thickly behind the centre of the barrier as to resemble heaps of fallen slates. Called out by police at 4.30am, with the storm still at its height, a woman supervisor worked right through to eight next evening, initially only by candlelight. Shoes were retrieved as far off as the Broadway. Apart from damage from falling timber, many local buildings lost roofs - a thousand on council properties alone - chimneys and windows, not to mention whole bus shelters picked up and thrown aside, or a massive advertising post at Westmoreland Place wrenched sideways into a drunken scarecrow, by winds believed to have touched 100mph. Three hundred council workmen were initially drafted in for road clearance, armed with about 150 bowsaws, 40 chainsaws and ten mechanical excavators. And that was just the beginning of clearing up.

Town centres were no more spared than open country. Library Gardens, when entered from Bromley High Street, today have a different look, with so many of the biggest trees gone. New vistas have opened, whereas before the storm little could be seen from the upper part of the Gardens of the Parish Church or the lake. One of the biggest trees has here slithered down the steep bank near the side restaurant entrance of the Churchill/Library block.

After-effects could be as simple as this, or something as internationally far-reaching as closure of the London Stock Exchange, for the first time since the 1974 devaluation crisis. Indirectly, therefore, our English storm is credited with being a contributory factor in Black Monday (only a few days after Hurricane Friday) when shares both sides of the Atlantic slumped in the biggest stock market fall since the Wall Street Crash.

Bromley Palace's serene facade is shown behind a curtain of anything but serene broken branches. Fortunately many of the ancient evergreens dating from its days as a bishop's palace, or as the Lord of the Manor's residence, emerged reasonably intact. But numbers of other majestic trees fell around the lake, whose scarred sites, ugly stumps, and the inevitable mud and ruts of clearance work, temporarily reduced the idyllic look of parts of the grounds in the spring of 1988.

Nature's nightmare, for a specially unlucky householder at Chelsfield. Not only was half the roof completely ripped off, with the gable end. The weakened back wall then collapsed onto the kitchen below, and in the process of wrecking the loft smashed open a 75-gallon cold water tank, a central heating tank, and a main. Thus, as if virtual blitzing were not enough, water flooded through the entire house, destroying almost all possessions. The final terror for the family was that as well as the roaring sound of the wind, it all happened in pitch darkness. Even then there was a final calamity to come: "We huddled under the stairs with our children aged 6 and 4. Fearing the whole house would fall in we decided to get to the garage - and a tree fell on that!". No wonder: only some four miles away, at Biggin Hill, a rock-bottom barograph figure of about 967mb was recorded at 4am.

Montage: The Great Storm as reported by the *Kentish Times* in Bromley borough.

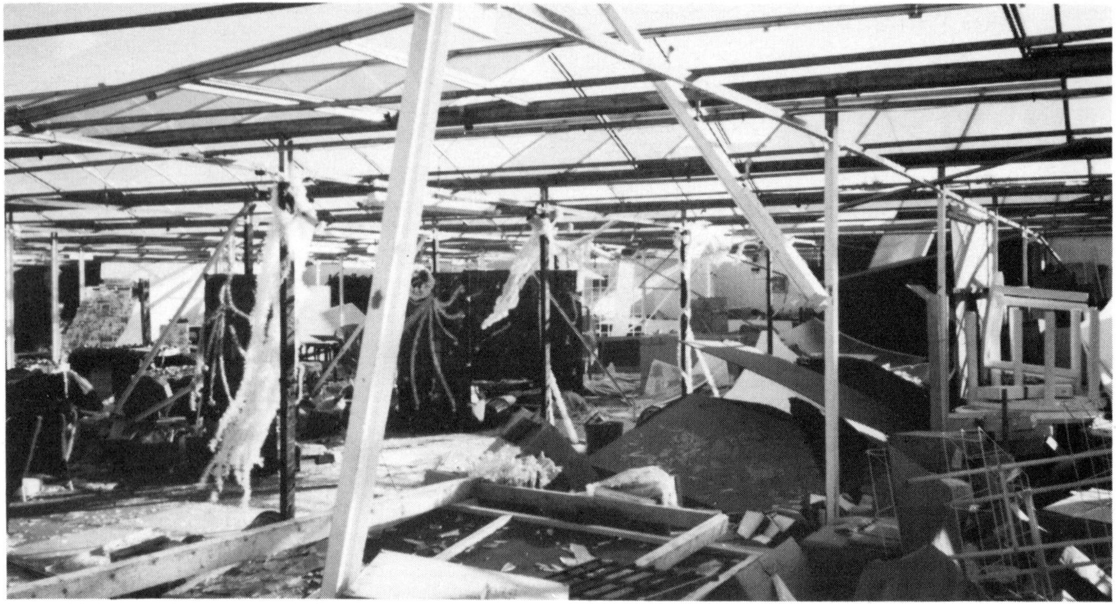

Only hours previously, false ceilings completely hid the greenhouse type glass roof of Polhill Garden Centre, turning it into an indoor shopping hall decorated that very day for approaching Christmas. A few remaining light tubes - one knocked sideways -identify where all trace of this ceiling vanished. Stock was flung into the foreground corner: drenched by rain through the glass-less roof, lying behind steel supports wrenched askew. One of the owners, in Tenerife on business, found several thousand other Britons at the airport seeking emergency flights home, so dramatic was the news.

With everything open to the sky at the garden centre, staff spent next night in sleeping bags, living off wine and cake from the coffee shop in a makeshift polythene-sheet dormitory, patrolling hourly by candle and lantern light. Eerie creakings from half-demolished buildings gave them an uneasy night. A reproduction furniture franchise suffered severe damage to its entire stock, needing sixteen journeys by truck to remove the remains. Final irony; the latter company's director, rejoicing that at least his car escaped any falling trees, saw an entire forklift truck's load of heavy pallets whipped off by a powerful gust and dumped upon it.

The new part of Farnborough churchyard some time after the hurricane, its crashed background little touched while more ugent clearance remained to be completed. Instead of scuttering up the standing trees, the author here noticed numerous squirrels running over the lying trunks. A *Kentish Times* reporter summed up the complete shift of feeling for trees and their inhabitants that one night of mayhem created, when, writing "a week after the funeral and cremation" of one huge beech. Only days before, he had bemoaned in his column the cheekiness of the squirrels, using nuts as ammunition to bombard him. "How I wish they could still perform that mischief. Now I would take the punishment gladly" he confessed. But the squirrels and the tree were both gone.

Historic masonry took a battering on Layhams Road at West Wickham, which was filmed by an early-bird cameraman at 7am on October 16. This massive tree growing inside the walled grounds of Wickham Court tore a top-to-bottom hole in this ancient wall despite it being, in the manner of Tudor builders, no less than five bricks thick. It also partly demolished a garden outhouse; not at the Court but on the opposite side of the road, so huge was the tree. Man's puniness is vividly captured, as a single person holding a small saw pits himself against this impossible-looking task. The trunk is so thick as to equal the distance between his feet and his elbows.

Genealogists calculate approximately three generations to an average century, thirty years apart. Therefore about nine or ten generations have passed since anyone in England experienced the sights that became commonplace in 1987. When this enormous tree outside what is now Hayes Library was a sapling, the first of those past generations would have been infants, hearing from their parents of the recent terrors of the Great Storm. Fallen complete forests on that scale have since been unknown until the visitation of "Len". One town near Bromley temporarily lost its very name; at Sevenoaks six out of the seven present-day namesake oaks were destroyed, prompting many a wag to suggest renaming it Oneoak.

Holwood House as we now know it was rebuilt after Pitt the great Prime Minister left; but the grounds keep many features he would have known, though now grown to considerable age. "Often have I seen him working in his woods and gardens with his labourers for whole days together" diarised one regular visitor. Another, Wilberforce, observed in 1790: "We sallied forth armed with bill-hooks, cutting new walks from one large tree to another through the thickets of the Holwood copses".

Any young trees they planted would have been two hundred year old veterans when they tumbled in 1987. Here a mammoth cedar lies as helpless as an axed seedling outside the mansion, confirming the domestic gardener's belief than any tree lying down is several times bigger than the same tree standing upright, when he faces removing its corpse. Such losses as this explain why Holwood House is now visible from afar, whereas previous views were restricted. Atop its commanding hill, it completes the Englishness of views from around Downe; one of the few cases of a proverbial ill-wind.

Figures compiled since October for the south-east (east of a diagonal line from Dorset to Norfolk) help underline the unique experience. Three thousand miles of collapsed telephone wires; 40% lost of all Essex cricket bat willows, an uncommon species otherwise grown mainly in Somerset; about £2,000,000 lost to British Rail on the train-lessSouthern Region; two leopards escaped from a Kent zoo; insurance claims first estimated at £500,000,000 and then revised again; half of a Sussex beach washed away, a recent man-made foreshore costing £12,000,000.

Bromley borough's losses came mainly from cars, house roofs and chimneys, fences and — of course — the trees. This being such a giant borough includes great areas of country, common and parkland. One interesting fact was that a tiny suburban park might lose, proportionately, as much timber as an estate like Scadbury, should the wind hit with full force. Husseywell at Hayes was a good example, both halves of this garden divided by a road being spectacularly wrecked. But this particular tree brought a spice of humour; broken off but caught almost horizontally above ground by several almost uniform length branches. The effect was of a many legged monster crawling from the Hayes jungle.

Ramblers could appreciate better than drivers, after fallen obstacles were cleared, the true extent of Kent's wounds. Deep in this wood beyond Farnborough is a typical example of how walkers for months after the storm found themselves lost in familiar territory. This particular path was blocked at the point pictured by at least seven trees lying close together. Taking evasive action around their roots only led woodland walkers farther than ever off route. The blasted effect of the background scene is also well conveyed. Again and again, witnesses compared the surviving but pitifully torn trees with pictures from the shelled Somme country in the First World War.

One of the wettest summers for years helped the wind do its worst. Leaf growth was extra thick, exposing maximum surface to the pushing wind; rather like an umbrella battered until blown inside-out. Additionally, roots had a loosened grip on their soil, which was abnormally damp and movable. Thirdly, many areas in Kent suffered a final deluge only days before; anything up to eight inches fell during that week. What chance was there for this unfortunate victim in Bourne Vale?.

Being aware that the author of "The War of the Worlds" was born in Bromley, people were quick to picture the machinery appearing on its streets as H G Wells' science fiction invaders. Steel jaws feeding on monster treetrunks did give that illusion. They also helped us appreciate for the first time the gigantic task facing the then tiny country village of Bromley when the last hurricane struck it, nearly three centuries before. Machinery like this, doing the work of whole teams of men and horses, would indeed have seemed like science fiction, back in 1703.

Interview by Kentish Times reporter

THE GREAT Storm was a night of fear for many — but for the Hall family it was a particularly horrific experience. Tony Hall is warden of the National Trust section of Petts Wood. His wife Madeleine is assistant warden. And the couple and their three children live in a cottage in a clearing inside the woodland itself.

He recalled: "We could hear tremendous cracks and crashes in the darkness all around us. As soon as one tree went it took others with it. Our youngest son, Barnaby, aged seven, was awake and very frightened."

Incredibly, the family's cottage did escape unscathed. But for Tony, who came to Petts Wood some six years ago, the worst was to come when he saw the dreadful damage to the wood that is "our work, our leisure and our whole way of life". He said "We were up before it was light. I remember I didn't want the morning to come, because of what we would find. "The destruction was indescribable, heartbreaking. Trees were down everywhere. We went outside to look at the damage and soon we were totally disorientated, we didn't know where we were, all the landmarks had gone. Just disappeared."

A huge number of trees were lost in the storm, some of them mature oaks up to 200 years old. In fact the oldest trees were often worst affected, because of their massive leaf area, which acted like sails to catch the wind.

Much of the devastation was visible to passers-by on nearby Chislehurst Road. But the most appalling destruction was hidden from drivers, deeper inside the woodland, between the Willett Stone and the Halls' cottage.

Petts Wood is probably the most important area of woodland in Bromley Borough. It dates far back to ancient times. About 330 acres of wood and farm land are administered by the National Trust. Another 180 acres are looked after by the Chislehurst and St Paul's Cray Commons Conservators. The two groups have already done much work, making the roadways safe for passing vehicles and removing fallen or dangerous trees from many woodland pathways. After the storm the area was so hazardous that the public were asked to keep away. But work is still continuing — the National Trust, for example, is employing a tree surgeon to assist Mr and Mrs Hall.

But only time can truly restore the woods to their former beauty, said Stanley Clayton, chairman of the National Trust's wood management committee.

He declared: "I have enjoyed walking in these woods all my life. Up until now, when you looked up you saw a canopy of branches - now there is an amazing amount of sky.

Apart from anything else, all that extra light on the woodland floor will change the environment. If we are not careful we will get a lot of soil erosion.

I think Petts Wood has been spoiled, without a doubt. But all is not lost - it will get back to health in many years' time. People who are young now will see the wood in its glory again, one day".

Opposite: Petts Wood before....

Opposite: Petts Wood after....

In normal times the occasional felled tree after a storm is no more than a nuisance. In modern England, the spectacle of a wall of foliage stretching the full width of a picture like this (at Bourne Vale) is unique to October 1987.

Bromley never looked like this before; Bromley scarcely existed last time there was a hurricane in England, far back in 1703. The shock of the night before shows on the faces of the handful of residents determined to get through on foot. Countless stories exist of people lost on land and sea, singing appropriate hymns to keep up their spirits. So what might be a likely choice for a suburb under a hurricane force gale? One 82-year-old man, living alone and with a lifelong fear of storms, told a visiting social worker next day: "I sang my favourite hymn: I need Thee, every hour I need Thee".

Lewes Road, Bromley, at a stage of partial clearance. The leaves and twigs have gone, the branches and trunk remain. Rather less remained of what, in its better days, had been a proudly maintained car. The "passenger" lolling across its back seat was a brawny one indeed.

Chaos comes to a neat and tidy little modern corner of Beckenham. Guttering off the centre house has been smashed off, and the "Private: Residents Only" sign wrenched away, together with the wall that crossed the roots of a tree. The borough was full of lucky householders whose property was damaged but not destroyed because several tons of trunk missed by feet, or even by inches. A quite average casualty was estimated to weigh about ten tons.

Normal features like a milk-float made the abnormality all the more striking; even unreal. Farnaby Road, Shortlands, was the archetypal residential street where hurricanes should not happen. Another strange feature was the air temperature in the middle of that dreadful night. Though within a fortnight of November, it was almost unnaturally warm despite the wind's ferocity. And because it was all so strange, ordinary people noticed extraordinary things with unusual precision; above all, the moment when all the lights went out. "It was 4.17am" reported an Orpington correspondent after rescuing her pet rabbit. Who, on any other day, would so exactly notice the time in the small hours?

Obstacle course near Badger's Mount

In the everyday suburban setting of Queen Anne Avenue, Shortlands, the sheer ordinariness of a milk float against the extraordinariness of trees blocking its path while cars edge past, gives this morning-after-the-night-before scene the impact of total contrast. Unfortunately some more unusual trees were lost in this road, including mature hornbeams, but the war memorial gardens just out of the picture planted in memory of air raid wardens killed when their wartime ARP post was bombed in the 1940s - leaving a hole big enough, it is said, to have held a 227 bus - luckily escaped almost unscathed.

It was interesting to discover how people living 284 years apart adopted almost identical expressions for describing the two English hurricanes. Defoe in 1703 repeatedly used the phrase "That terrible night". In conversation, by far the commonest words used in 1987 were "that awful night".

"In London, and especially in the out-parts (suburbs)... nothing can be said sufficient to describe it"; even Defoe the expert wordsmith was defeated. We all felt the same inadequacy of words when trying to convey Hurricane Len to people in the unaffected counties. "No pen can describe it; no tongue can express it; no thought conceive it unless...in the extremity of it", was another Defoe phrase.

The 1987 counterpart was the disbelief of people elsewhere that England should suffer such a thing; near neighbours of the author received telephone calls from Canada, the USA, New Zealand and Australia within a few hours, so dramatic was the news when received so far away. This scene in Rochester Avenue, Bromley, sums up the unreality of a hurricane in suburbia.

"Well; now what do we do?" Hayes suburbians confer against a background of two collapsed trees, a drunken telegraph pole, a trapped car, and sagging wires. As for thousands of others, the commonplace saying "under a tree" had graphic new meaning. So did the equally simple expression "raising the roof", for nearby Bromley Football Club. Their Saturday fans had no chance to raise the roof; Friday's wind had done it for them. However, Bromley took revenge on the wind by beating Kingstonian 2-0. Four supporters had spent the afternoon clearing rubble plus part of the smashed perimeter fence off the pitch. The club also lost lighting for training, and the turnstiles were lifted right out of their parent brickwork.

CONWAY
LTD.
01 676 0022

Opposite

Man-made suburban orderliness when violently disturbed by nature in chaos seemed to have special impact. It was all so utterly divorced from our lifetimes' conception of what suburbia ought to be. But here is chaos as far as the eye can see, the length of a normally quite ordinary residential road.

OCTOBER 16th, 1987

My house is called "Woodlands" and is in Chislehurst. Until October last year, my garden was surrounded by trees.

The Lead Up.

1.30am I woke up and there was a strong gale blowing at about 50-60mph.

2.00am The wind was roaring now. This was when the hurricane was really starting here.

2.30am Wood started cracking, but nothing yet had actually fallen.

3.00-4.00am A few trees were falling in that hour, but mostly it was branches. At 4.00 the wind seemed to be at its highest.

The Happening

4.00am I heard a smashing of glass. Our neighbour's greenhouse had turned on its side in the wind.

4.14am I looked out of my window again. Our other neighbour's willow tree was still there, but his Scots Pine and Beech had blown into our garden with a huge noise.

4.20am The oak tree in the middle of my garden was left unprotected now. It started to lean.

4.25am The oak tree is leaning more and more.

4.30am I looked out again. The oak tree started collapsing. The ground seemed to disappear. The huge tree smashed towards the ground, and the ground below it lifted up.

Conclusion

Most of the damage was done between 4.00-4.45am. But in under 4 hours trees and other things hundreds of years old were destroyed. Our tree surgeon said our tree weighed about 6 tons.

Nicholas Bradley, 9 years.

A scene at the top of Wickham Court Court, West Wickham, near the traffic lights, with wreckage blocking both sides until this tractor had done its work. Apart from local authority work at points like this, there was a huge amount of clearance to be done on private property. One of the first facts to emerge was the general public's concern not just to clear their own gardens, but also to restore the Borough's ruined beauty. Not only did the Thousand Tree Appeal bring in far greater response than was initially imagined. Ordinary people were so anxious to handle their damaged trees correctly and save what they could, or to plant those replacements standing the best chance of flourishing, that the booklet "Damaged Trees: What to do after the Great Storm" virtually walked off the library's counters; the writer needed to pay several visits to strike a time between arrival of new supplies and yet another emptied counter.

A Bourne Vale, Hayes, example of unexpected booby-traps, apart from the obvious fallen branches. Cables embedded in roots as a tree grew had been dragged out of the earth when it fell. There is also very characteristic opening up of adjacent paving slabs, akin to a sardine can being prised open. In the country, similarly, distinctive features became new landmarks to replace bushes and trees that formerly identified each path and branching off point; an unusually shaped stump, a distorted trunk, or the way a tree fell halfway and was caught and held in the branches of another. These were useful identifications, until they in turn were cleared away, leaving the scene as bereft of landmarks as at the start; for example, the temporarily almost featureless bulldozed desert above the banks of Old Hill.

Wickham Court Road with the most obliging tree in the district. It scarcely touched the left-hand gate and left both gateposts intact as it fell neatly through the open half of this double gate, over the road, and into another open gate opposite. It also missed two parked cars. It reminds us of another incident with an evergreen, whose owners spent several hours taking turns, after hauling it upright on ropes, to hold it there. Only some time towards bedtime did it dawn on them that eventually they would need to let go; a contest which the tree, of course, won.

Remaining with storm anecdotes; we were told of a school child asked what he thought was the most frightening or unforgettable thing about living through an all-night hurricane. Was it the darkness? The noise of thrashing and crashing trees? The power of the wind? A world of fallen tiles, blown-off roofs, wrecked cars and collapsed trees wherever he went? None of these. The greatest disaster was lack of electricity to power the most dominant thing in a modern child's life: "We couldn't even watch a video"!

He shared his lack with 3,999,999 others, as four million were estimated to be without power at the worst point. Despite the long hours worked by 4,000 Seeboard staff backed up by volunteers, about 49,000 in the South-East were still disconnected next day; another criterion by which to measure the unprecedented scale of the storm. A week after, over 1,500 men, including Forces personnel, were still clearing local fallen power lines buried in debris.

Outside this garage in The Drive, Beckenham, a jungle of branches blocked any hope of escape. Leaves can be seen forcing their way into the half opened door and through the sagging roof. Four men worked for six hours before the car could be moved out, from under two massive trees.

In its prime this was a driveable BMW. A very large sycamore in Holbrook Lane, Chislehurst, not only flattened its roof, but also pierced it at several points with jagged and splintered branches. It was regarded as "a local tourist attraction" for a full week afterwards.

The average Bromleian would never have imagined that Hurricane Floyd, starting over the far Caribbean and then edging up the Florida coast, had any relevance here. When it collided off the US East Coast with colder Polar air as a 200mph "jet streak" and then turned out over the Atlantic, it was still only of meteorological interest. So was a large depression off Brittany, even though one of its strange effects of dramatic temperature contrasts was noted near home. About four hours before the storm dubbed Hurricane Len struck, the night temperature in Essex was only 7 degrees C (45 degrees F); not far off in Kent it topped a freakish 18 degrees C (64 degrees F), at ten on an October night.

This, compared with pressure dropping past thunderstorm level and still plunging, puzzled few ordinary people, giving their home barometers the usual perfunctory tap before going to bed. Finally the "jet streak" and the Brittany depression met and created a certain form of rain to explode a natural "bomb".

It was at the point after this when the barometer first began rising again, that winds reached their greatest speed. At the two ends of our home county, London experienced its highest-ever recorded wind force of 94mph; and at Dover it reached an average of 85mph, not only as gusts but also including the minimum of ten continuous minutes required to be accepted as Hurricane Force, or Force Twelve - plus another 12mph above that level.

No wonder this was the most universal sight throughout Bromley Borough next day (A scene at Bourne Vale, Hayes.)

A lurking creature peers out of the Bourne Vale jungle, just its eyes and mouth visible among the dense foliage. Or were they two headlights and a number plate? Because virtually every citizen had seen a tree victim like this at close hand, in their own roads, the appeal quickly started to raise the cost of at least some replacements inspired great generosity; it had personal meaning, near home. Thus over £3,000 came in during the first fortnight alone of the Thousand Tree Appeal, sponsored by Bromley Council and the Kentish Times with the Mayor as patron; on average £150 a day to start with, and double that in the second week. The first nursery-grown saplings were bought while the branches of their predecessors were still everywhere lying on the ground.

Never since motoring began has a car squashed by a tree, in such spectacular fashion as this, been such a commonplace sight that somebody walking the dog in Bourne Vale seems not to bother even to look at it. Had the winds struck twelve hours earlier or later, however, many would undoubtedly have become their drivers' tombs. On the other hand, night darkness intensified the sense of fear, and also brought out the long forgotten "Battle of Britain spirit". Not far from the former Battle of Britain airfield of Biggin Hill an 83-year-old man (C T Bird) has described going out at 4am, when most of us were unashamedly cowering in bed, and helped retrieve the wreckage of a neighbour's fence; then went on to check the safety of two elderly women, walking to their home by candlelight in a gale still strong enough to blow out the fires of Hades.

THE STORM

Bang goes the gate,
There goes the crate flying down the lane.
Crash, smash, Oh no! Now it's the window pane.
Lying in bed listening to the horrible wind
The horrible whistling, whooshing wind
The wind that damages everything.
Clang goes the dustbin lid against the trees
Not just a normal little breeze.
The trees fall down like a domino rally
And the whistling wind down the alley.
The howling wind goes on all night
And then, Oh no! Out goes the light.
The banging and clanging soon will stop,
And everyone will have a busy job.
That moaning, groaning horrible wind
That rips off tiles and everything.
The howling wind goes on all night,
It's enough to give anything a fright.
Crash, smash, a tree falls on the house
It goes straight through the window and lands on my mouse.
It rips holes in the roof,
That let the rain in
Soon we will be able to go for a swim.
That crashing, smashing horrible wind
The wind that damaged everything.

by Emma Richmond, aged 10, Pupil at Princes Plain Primary School.

But for the presence of the modern mast, this could almost be taken for the morning after the Crystal Palace fire in 1936, with smouldering rubble across the terraces above the sphinxes guarding the stately staircase. But this rubble was timber instead of stone, iron and glass.

This vehicle had cost a local councillor about £2,000 secondhand only a few months before Hurricane Len reduced it to a glorified tin can, as it roared over the Monks Orchard area of Beckenham. Complete with the main trunk of the embedded tree, it was put on public display, including two days at the Civic Centre exhibition. It is a very good example of the effect known to the general public as a squashed car; put on show, it brought home to many people the loss of life that would undoubtedly have occurred had the storm struck in daytime.

Never having seen tree after tree lying prone — and neither had nine or ten generations before us — few people had realised how shallow were their roots. One instinctively imagined giant tap roots probing deep down, proportionate to the growth above ground. Small wonder that, after one of the wettest so-called summers for years, helping loosen the soil, they had so little grip against winds of up to Force 12. A good example bridges Halstead Lane, Halstead.

Normally the only days of the year without trains are Christmas Day and Boxing Day; for we who live alongside the main line through Bromley, to be trainless at any other time feels strange, silent and almost eerie. Thus the sense of unreality on October 16 was heightened by total emptiness on the line. British Rail was faced with a truly unprecedented situation; how to remove not one fallen tree (an occasional hazard needing a full gang for clearance), but hundreds. Near the Kent/Sussex border, 74 lay across one two and a half mile stretch. In our own borough the reopening of all lines by the following Monday's rush-hour was a feat of physical endurance; not only against wreckage but also the resulting inches-thick gooey plaster of wet shed leaves, compacted onto the rails. Even on Friday itself, some sections were reopened, notably on the Charing Cross to Orpington parts. *Kentish Times* estimated the fallen trees on the little Hayes to Elmers End branch at over 150; an incredible average of fifty trees to the mile. Additionally, the holes they left weakened parts of the embankments, dislodging loose earth and stones to further litter the track. This view from a road bridge at Westgate Road, near Beckenham Junction, shows men at work on one of the less badly blocked sections; at any other time, a tree like this on the main line would form a major problem.

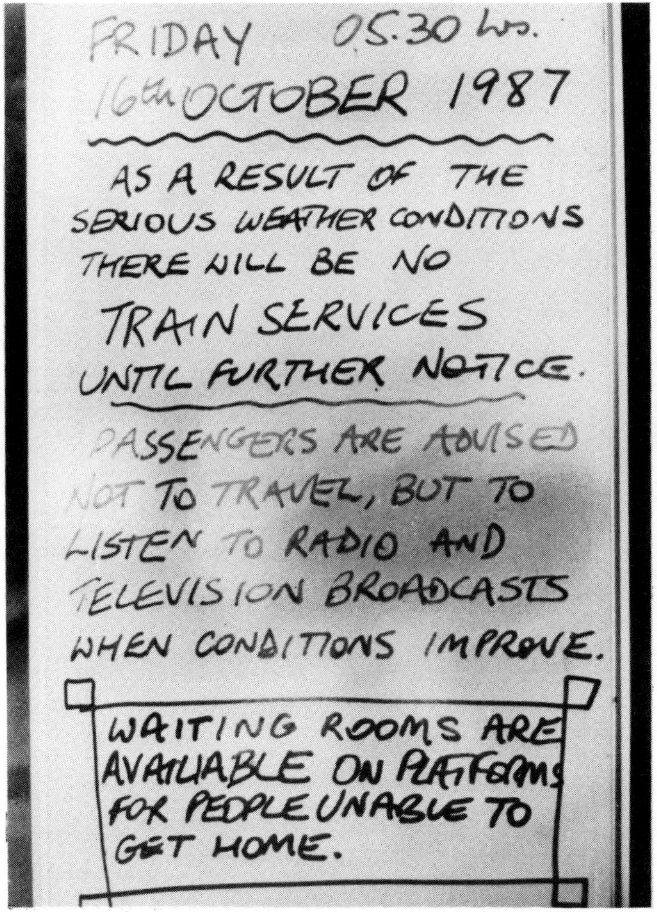

As early as 5.30am it was already obvious that no trains could run anywhere in the South East. There was thus an almost wartime character to the tail-piece of this station notice about camping out in waiting rooms. Even Hitler never achieved such a universal cessation of all trains as did Mother Nature's blitz.

Before-and-after pictures are acceptable in enough cosmetics advertising, illustrating that the product will transform an ordinary woman into a beauty. When nature goes wrong outdoors, they are the reverse: beauty transformed into ugliness; or, at least, far removed form the original scene. Here the writer's mother sits on a favourite fallen log, in the days when one of these was a rare boon to walkers instead of the commonest countryside feature of all. Behind her are the top few trees of Beechy Walk, the only ones spared by the storm, and the massively thick flanking woods.

This companion shot was taken only a few yards from the earlier one, again showing the remaining Beechy Walk trees. The rest of the forest is almost eaten away, but for a thin shaggy fringe of timber across the hilltop fence. Beyond that — nothing.

Bromley Parish church (St Peter and St Paul) in high summer with surrounding trees. The restored medieval tower blended with the newer but traditionally styled nave into a composition that could be a million miles from London — or hurricane country.

After final clearance of dead wood and fallen trunks, the Parish Church stared across a bleak, denuded landscape. Apart from the evergreens which, having more flexibility and give, generally were best equipped to survive, only one of the old surrounding trees was left. Shorn, like countless others, of so much timber as to resemble a very tall and thin skeleton.

This churchyard was one of the worst littered in the diocese, with several massive trees felled across the graves. It was many weeks before the final branches were removed, so much had come down. This tree and one or two companions near the railings dividing the churchyard from Church House Gardens also dragged sections of this fencing up from the ground, as their roots moved.

Interview by Kentish Times reporter

NICK Ditchburn and Derek Coad were the first council workers on the scene for the night of the Great Storm.

The pair were summoned from their beds at 1.30am in the morning, to deal with an uprooted shrub blocking Church Lane, Chelsfield. They were to spend the next 18 hours on the job.

Nick, who is an assistant forester with Bromley Council, said: "We were never scared, we just got on with it — but a couple of times we did have to dive under the lorry".

Nick recalled: "I hadn't seen the weather forecast and was sleeping through the howling winds before the first callout.

By around 2.30am the winds were really gusting and to get to each new job we were having to clear two or three trees along the route".

In that first hour Nick and Derek, who is an arborist, had moved fast and cleared trees from Chislehurst Road, Bromley Road, Walden Avenue and Yester Road, Chislehurst — where one tree had fallen onto a car.

But it was then that street lights were blacked out as power lines went down, and in pitch darkness the two worked along Lubbock Road and Old Hill, clearing trees as they went.

Nick said: "By the time we reached Bromley Road, which runs through the wood at Chislehurst, things were really hairy. There were loud cracks all around us, and we couldn't tell where they were coming from.

A couple of times we had to dive under the lorry and eventually a tree fell on to the lorry. Enough was enough. We retired back to the cricket ground. The wind was rocking the cab, but at least there were no trees!" Amazingly, Nick and Derek had to turn back

several cars trying to drive down Bromley Road and through the woods in the next couple of hours.

Nick said: "Some people told us they were trying to reach a place of safety, but I think they were going the wrong way about it."

It took the two until 11am to clear Bromley Road alone. They spent the next few days dealing mostly with trees that had fallen onto houses. Until heavy lifting cranes could be brought in, that meant propping up the trunks with wood blocks and removing branches to lighten the load as much as possible. The worst damaged properties in the borough were probably in Tower Road and Hawfield Bank, Orpington.

Damage from the Great Storm has been dealt with in order of the danger posed to the public - and has kept council workers hard at work. Their wives have dubbed themselves "tree widows". Nick, for example, had only had two and a half proper days off in the six months after the hurricane winds. But he said: "I'm glad I was involved, because, in years to come, I can tell people: I was there."

Few pictures could be more heartbreakingly telling of Bromley's loss than this placid view of Beechy Walk at High Elms, Farnborough, in maturity. On a summer day, the precisely-spaced trunks' shadows took the eye off into an infinite distance. Horse riders used to amble up through the shade on this straight way through otherwise dense woods. Now the woods are gone, for great distances on either side; and over the rest of the hill from its brow to its foot; and nearly all of Beechy Walk itself. The spring of 1988, when clearance was going towards a close, left only a vast space of nothingness, barren and brown and bare, bereft of all growth, littered only with shorn off stumps and a few scattered logs. That is the difference between the most violent of gales and a hurricane that strikes only once in three hundred years.

The tragedy of Beechy Walk in one dreadful picture. Only a few trees were left, initially standing above a virtual gorge, in miniature, composed of pairs of root clumps looking like giant boulders. Temporarily, the wildness was almost beautiful, had it not been so sad.

Standing in line as if about to take a normal uphill walk, this photographer found a combination of upended stumps at Beechy Walk, white with Kentish chalk, and the once-stately trunks flung at right-angles across them.

The sum total of the trees that were spared: a very minor kindness from Mother Nature, in allowing posterity a small idea of what the complete Walk might have looked like. Beyond the last trees are the first cut stumps. However, plans were revealed in May 1988 for eventually replanting the Walk on its old site. The worst wreckage had gone by early 1988, making possible these ephemeral views of the Beechy Walk site before final disappearance. The only remaining trees, about fifty, stood exposed on the hilltop, but the line of the entire walk was still marked by a double line of stumps spaced in pairs exactly as they were, each upended to face the same direction.

Farnborough floored; all facing the same way according to the wind direction.

Approaching the stage of final clearance, with only stumps left on the ground. Horse riders in the spring of 1988 gave a contradictory air of normality in abnormal surroundings, by following as closely as possible their old favourite ride through the length of Beechy Walk. Unable to take the actual line of the Walk, still a confusion of upended stumps, they were riding alongside it.

Husseywell Gardens at Hayes were closed to the public for some weeks whilst acting as a trees' crematorium. This scene was filmed about five weeks after the great storm, apparently with much work still to be done. Kent in general was among the three worst hit counties (with Sussex and Suffolk), losing on average 20% of all trees; some sites, naturally, were far above average as at Toys Hill or Chartwell, with up to 80% lost. One would expect far less damage to London, the great urban capital; yet even there, in parks and streets, the loss was no less than 250,000 trees.

Not since the 1940s Blitz did local photographers have such wide scope for then-and-now filming. In the older picture Farnborough is the quintessential English countryside, under large mature trees.

The “now” scene on the same footpath shows a specially common effect, where a tree has survived, but stripped bare of almost all its side limbs and branches except for a few scruffy and mis-shapen fragments at the very top; not unlike the current breed of tall skinny punk with his topknot of unkempt spikey hair. Pines in particular suffered this treatment.

October 16th, 1987.

Wind moaning
Gales lashing
Windows rattling
Windows shattering
Houses shaking
Poles swaying
Trees toppling
Trees crashing
How are the mighty fallen!
It lies there, a broken giant,
Great roots torn from the earth,
Wrenched from the soil by huge unseen hands.
How it must have cried as it fell,
With no time to plead for its life.
Over a hundred years of growth
Pulled down in a moment of fury.
No more will birds hide in the leaves
Or squirrels climb the highest branches.
No more will children play in its shade,
Or lovers whisper at dusk in its cover
No more will it put forth the new green leaves in the Spring,
Or shower the ground in the autumn with pure gold.
Oh capricious wind! Just see what you've done.
No reason, no motive, no possible good.
A glorious tree just reduced to mere wood.
Oh God! Who created each tree to delight,
How could You — why did You — allow such a wind
To shatter completely this beautiful thing?
Majestic in life —
Majestic in death.
So be it — Amen.

Beth Fender.

A very characteristic effect recorded at Queen's Mead, Shortlands. A tree was left standing but with its entire top part twisted round and snapped off, rather like disbudding a chrysanthemum. The snapped-off section, instead of falling, would be caught and firmly held in a lower branch or fork. This one remained hanging upside-down for many weeks, apparently safe enough to be left while more dangerous trees were being felled.

Old Hill as it looked in its normal state, one of the loveliest and leafiest lanes of the district. But on Wednesday, October 14, a steady barometer suddenly plunged into its first downward drop. On the 15th it took a second ominous nosedive, prognosticating something very unusual to come. Then, soon after midnight, it swooped down for a third and final time, into the climax of the winds that destroyed Old Hill, Church Road, and High Elms. The final interesting point was a close parallel with the ending of the Great Storm of 1703 when Defoe observed: "It was very tempestuous all the morning; at one o'clock the wind abated...and by four o'clock there was not a breath of wind." After holding at rock bottom for less than two hours, the barograph line climbed out of the trough almost vertically, and by nightfall on October 16th was almost back to average.

Only by walking up on foot rather than driving in a car is it possible to fully appreciate the total destruction of Old Hill, whose new bleakness became more particularly apparent after the tangled masses of wreckage were removed. Even they were some form of cover; now there is virtually nothing left. Clearance was in its last stages when this shot was taken in March 1988, looking upwards to the top of the High Elms ridge. It is now most difficult, on foot and with time to stare, to associate this particular sight with what one had known before: a deeply sunken English lane, twisting and turning through a tunnel of leaves almost meeting overhead.

Post-hurricane Farnborough ended its sorry saga as a massive lumber camp, the temporarily familiar sight of countless fallen trees replaced by another newly universal feature: heaps of sawn logs towering above the heads of ramblers, or passing cars. An entire copse is here lying by the roadside on Old Hill. Exposed Kentish chalk in these parts increased the sensation of gaunt desolation, shining so white and so blank compared wiht the former gentle green.

This is a particularly telling pair of pictures showing a site before and after the hurricane, taken in the field behind St Giles' church at Farnborough, looking towards the High Elms ridge. One is a perfect English summer scene, with the thick woods sheltering the Lubbock graves on the left.

Some time after the great storm the photographer stood on the identical spot for this spectacular comparative illustration of wind power, with only a handful of pines left standing. The rest is more suggestive of the aftermath of an Australian bush fire, seen here on television, than peaceful Farnborough. Inside the woods the drama was even clearer; such a tangle of wreckage that identifying a familiar footpath was difficult six months later. The devastation stretched right through to the once-beautiful Church Road on the far side.

On public roads, the two worst transformations occured in the same vicinity; Old Hill and Church Road at Farnborough. Church Road as here seen bears very little resemblance to the bare and hard embankments that were left after all the destroyed trees were cleared away, particularly at the lower end where it approached High Elms.

By waiting for cars to appear, the photographer was able to convey the scale of Church Road at Farnborough after first the wind and then the clearance gangs had finished with it. A few weeks earlier it was one of our loveliest treelined roads, forming a tunnel of green that was just turning to gold when the gale struck. So severe was the destruction here and throughout the wide strip of woods above, that no semblance of normality remained. This bare excavated embankment, gleaming with scraped-off chalk and almost devoid of new growth, sums up the heartbreak that was Farnborough.

A healthy young oak tree, planted in 1952, is seen growing up inside the hollow trunk of the dying original Wilberforce Oak at Holwood, Keston, before final removal of the old enclosing railings. A few years after this picture was taken, it was even stronger and more flourishing, at about 35 years old, and the surrounding trunk that was actually known to Wilberforce was just a rotting carcase. Yet it was the strong young tree that crashed and the battered hulk that survived, with little additional reduction in size.

Wilberforce Oak II was given by Seismograph Service, present owners of Holwood, to be sliced up into just one hundred pieces, sold at £2 each during the Hurricane Exhibition in aid of replacement tree planting in the Borough. With each slice went this explanatory certificate quoting an extract from Wilberforce's diary. It is hoped that, when more important clearance work is finished, a Wilberforce Oak III may be formally planted at the same spot.

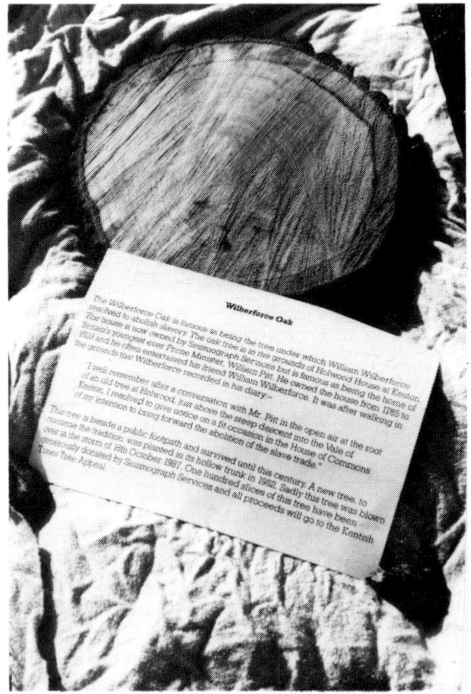

Mother Nature laughed at Holwood. Not long before the storm the stone commemorative seat facing Wilberforce Oak (inscribed with the story of how abolition of slavery dated from a conversation beneath its shade between Pitt and Wilberforce) was moved off the public footpath. In its place was put the more ordinary seat seen nearest the camera, and the precious historic relic resited in a "safer" place behind the fence. Nature, in fact, laughed twice. Once when the vigorous-looking young second Wilberforce Oak, growing inside the wreck of the original tree, crashed down leaving the latter defiantly standing upright. Twice, when the uprooted younger tree fell exactly across the seat in its new place, completely missing the site where it normally would have been. Fortunately there was no special damage. The stone seat can be seen half buried in fallen foliage behind the wire fence.

Before...The picturesque "old oak lich-gate" into the hilltop church of St John The Baptist at West Wickham. Until the 1920s it was still divorced from its parent settlement, then consisting simply of Wickham Street "a pleasant quiet cluster of country cottages about a green". In the more trustworthy world of the 1960s the author recalls staff and clergy using the broad under-roof crossbeam as a depository for the church keys, left there for the first one to arrive for the next service.

After. . . Remains of West Wickham lich-gate, or lych-gate, stacked up beside its original site. A rough patch at right shows where the hole left by the tree that destroyed it was roughly filled in. At left are the two main side supports, with the reasonably intact roof structure, with a few smashed tiles still trapped inside. Not crushed by a tree, it was dragged over and into the hole as the adjacent tree's spreading roots were forced up underneath it, collapsing the nearest supporting beams. So many other trees fell that the entire setting was changed. Instead of huddling into a soft circle of foliage, the church is now harshened and exposed, especially as seen from Coney Hall; almost fortress-like when seen against lowering clouds or approaching dusk, rather than soothing to the eye as it was before.

Woodman, don't spare that tree; it was far past sparing when Hurricane Len had finished with it. However, domestic DIY enthusiasts and gardeners were repeatedly warned against tackling jobs like this themselves, due to the unpredictability of a haphazardly felled tree. Shorn of the first few supporting limbs, they tended suddenly to roll or collapse in a highly dangerous manner. We witnessed one tree at Petts Wood with no less than three large saws embedded, unable to be used, after an unexpected movement, even with a professional team.

Palace View, Bromley: the clearing-up operation begins.

High-lying Biggin Hill felt the full force of wind across the exposed airport. Eight aircraft were damaged, being near falling trees, four being virtual write-offs. One was broken into two separate halves, as if attacked with a giant axe. Other freak effects included fires at some houses in Hayes when returning current sent power surges through their electrical sytems.

No use waiting for a bus today:— a main road at Biggin Hill on the morning-after-the-night-before.

Smoking wreckage that once was the borough's trees. Early days of clearance work at Green Street Green.

Visiting Cator Park, Beckenham, the Mayor was photographed with clearance workers armed with a lethal-looking selection of tree cutting tools.

The sort of lucky shot that a photographer can rarely actually plan. The author reached the gardens round Hayes Library when gardeners were in the act of planting a young sapling close to one of the biggest casualties in the borough. The enormous size of this tree, estimated to be about three hundred years old, was therefore given a very telling scale against three human beings and a frail young sapling. It was already intended to put another cedar or similar tree close to this site; initially smaller and more ornamental trees were bought, being cheaper. Cash for a new cedar was raised by members of Hayes Afternoon Townswomen's Guild, to celebrate their 35th birthday. By Spring of 1988 it was installed and flourishing.

This "hurricane sculpture" arranged outside a motor showroom on Masons Hill created great public interest and amusement by its ingenuity in using so many aspects of the destruction, together with the shape of young growth to come. Around the inevitable flattened car underneath the treetrunk that destroyed it, can be spotted heaps of wood chippings, twisted branches, trailing ivy, a section through a very large smashed tree, evergreens that escaped, and several new ex-nursery saplings. As well as attracting many onlookers, this display also publicised some of the earliest efforts in raising cash for replanting our devastated borough.

Children of Princes Plain School with acorns for replanting collected off a destroyed tree in the gardens; an unexpected way of teaching practical natural history. Characteristically, the children's observations recorded at another school ranged from a blasé opinion of computers ("weather men blame a computer for not telling them about this hurricane") to the utterly basic: "Our roof is leaking because the tiles have fallen off".

Ramblers starting from Cuckoo Wood car park for High Elms, in March 1988, were dwarfed by walls of cut timber, piled up as clearance work got under way. Smaller pieces on private land were sometimes turned to more commemorative use, cut up for garden seats, bird tables and picnic furniture. The £2 slices of the second Wilberforce Oak, sold at the Trees For Tomorrow Exhibition, made attractive tops for outdoor stools. And one small piece of treetrunk became a chairman's gavel holder, inscribed simply "Great Storm 1987", for Bromley Probus Club.

One of the happier factors was the speed with which rehabilitation began, without waiting first to clear all evidence of the storm. Bromley would be green again, seemed to be the message of this contradictory moment at Petts Wood, when a new tree was being planted while stumps and shed twigs of its predecessor still lay alongside.

An appropriate title for a picture like this, in H G Wells's home town, might be taken from one of his lesser known books: "Anticipations". In contrast to the chaos of destruction, this was the chaos of reconstruction, as young tree saplings came in to Church House Gardens ready for distribution around the worst damaged sites in the borough.

A public demonstration of tree clearing machinery, outside the Civic Centre during the Trees for Tomorrow Exhibition, popularly simply the Hurricane Exhibition. It brought home the huge difference between 1703, when in Kent 17,000 trees had to be laboriously cut up with simple hand tools, and 1987 when a whole trunk fed into this machine could be reduced to mere sawdust in a few seconds. The sawdust can be seen shooting from the tall funnel outlet directly into a waiting open lorry.

The public showed much enthusiasm for the superb Trees For Tomorrow Exhibition in January 1988, crowding in not only to see the displays and the aerial video, but also in the spirit of laying a ghost. It acted as a formal ending, with its forward-looking theme of tomorrow's Bromley, clean and green again. Jazz bands helped put the gloom to flight. About fifteen thousand people attended during the two days, including those who had worked so hard on initial rehabilitation.

ROLL OF HONOUR

This is the Roll of Honour for those who made donations to the Kentish Times and Bromley Borough Council Thousand Tree Appeal. At the time of going to press, contributions were still coming in.

Abacus Elfins of the Woodcraft Folk.
Abbott, Patrick and Vivien.
Abrehart, family.
Abson, Mr and Mrs W.W.
Abson, S.M.
Abson, Stephanie.
Abson, Vivien
Adams, Mrs J.
Addison, P.G.
Aird, Mr and Mrs J.H.
Aird, Mrs Marjorie
Alexandra Infants School, Beckenham.
Allaway, Mr and Mrs W.
Allen, E.H.
Allen, Patricia.
Allen, Rita.
Allwright, C.
Ambrose, family of Orpington.
Anderson, Mr and Mrs J.
Andrew, Jean.
Andrew, Mrs C. In memory of her late husband William Andrew.
Andrews, Ms Olive
Anonymous donation in memory of Nurse Marie Wilson of Enniskillen and victims of the Remembrance Day tragedy.
Anstey, C.
Archer, A.R.
Archibald, Margaret.
Armitage, Nicole.
Arnheim, Wendy.
Arnold, Dr and Mrs R.
Arnold, Mrs Juliet. In memory of her daughter, Linda.
Asherson, Jean.
Ashford, Mrs A.
Aspland, Ron and Beryl.
Aste Mr C W
Avitel Electronics Ltd, of Beckenham.
Aylott, D
Babbage, Edith.
Babington House School.
Baggaley, H.
Bailey, Dorothy and Herbert.
Bailey, Mr and Mrs Herbert.
Baillie, Mrs. In memory of her husband.
Baker, L.R. and D.A.
Baker, Margaret.
Baker, Miss Patricia Ann,
Baker, Patricia.
Bamji, Alexandra and Nicholas.
Bansome Wood Stables, riders.
Barat,Janet M.
Barker family of West Wickham, in memory of Sidney.
Barnard, J.E.
Barnes, Alan.
Barnes family of Orpington.
Barnes, Mrs P. In memory of her mother, Doris Robinson.
Barret, Janet.
Barrett, J.S.
Barton, Mr and Mrs A.R.
Bassett, Mr & Mrs G.
Bass, Mrs.
Beacon, Mr and Mrs C.A.
Beale, Adrienne
Bearman, Mrs M.G.
Beasley, Mr and Mrs.
Beckenham Co-Op Keep Fit and Dance Group.

Beckenham Manor (Afternoon) Townswomen's Guild's gardening section.
Beckenham Woodcraft Elfins Group.
Beckenham Co-Op Community Council.
Beckenham Central Townswomen's Guild.
Beckenham Women's Institute.
Beckenham Co-op Mothers, Toddlers Group.
Beckenham Baptist Church.
Beckenham Co-Op Playgroup.
Beckwith, Lesley Anne.
Beechwood Residents' Association, Farnborough.
Beer, Mr and Mrs T.A.
Bell, M.F.
Bell, Mr and Mrs P.L.
Bennett, A.
Benscher, Mrs E.M.
Benson, M.V.
Beresford House School, Bromley, pupils and staff.
Beresford, William.
Berry, H.E.
Berry, H F.
Berry, H.G. and Dr A.A.Thornton.
Berry, Jane.
Berry, June
Berry, Mrs E.K. In memory of her late father, William Smith.
Berry, Mrs K.
Bertoli, Mr and Mrs Dennis.
Betts, Mr and Mrs L.V.
Beveridge, J.
Bickley Women's Institute.
Biddlecombe, V.
Bidmead, Mrs J.P.
Biggin Hill Women's Institute.
Biggin Hill (Evening) Women's Institute.
Biggs, Rita, June and Margaret.
Bird, Anthony, Marguerite and Carol.
Bird, Chas T.
Bird, Madeline.
Bishop, Clara, Jeremy, Janet and Colin.
Bishop, Mrs S. In memory of Mrs Letitia Mary Harris and Mrs Grace Kinnibrugh.
Bishop, Mr and Mrs A.
Bishop, Mr.
Blackaby, Paul D.
Blackburn, Eileen.
Black, Mr and Mrs A.R.
Blackwall, Sarah.
Blackwell, Sarah in memory of Arthur Tregent.
Blackwell, H.E.
Blake, Michael.
Blake, Mr and Mrs.
Blaney, Mr & Mrs Arthur.
Blaxill, Mrs G.E.
Blaxill, Mr & Mrs G E.
Blenheim Infants School, Orpington.
Blenheim Junior School, Orpington.
Bluetit Patrol, 3rd Mottingham (St Andrew's) Guide Company.
Blundell, Mr and Mrs J.J.G.
Bolton, Mr and Mrs K.
Bonham, Mary.
Boorman, Mr and Mrs R.A.
Booth, Joyce and George.
Booth, Mrs L.
Booth-Smith, J.G.
Bowers, Sampson P.
Boyd, Miss J. In memory of Bess, Clark, Terry, Joyce, Christine, Simon and Vincent, Cluny, and guide dog Timber.
Bracon, Mr & Mrs.
Bradley, C.E.
Bradshaw, Mr and Mrs A.R.
Brafield, Dr and Mrs F.
Brand, Mrs.
Brassett, Mr and Mrs G.H.
Bratton, Mrs P.M.
Brehart, A & Family.
Breuner, R.
Brice, N.R.

Bridgeman, Mrs M.C.
Bridger, L.E. and G.E.
Bristol Street Motors Ltd.
British Red Cross Society, Beckenham, Penge and West Wickham Centre.
Broadwood, David.
Brockett, John and Margaret.
Brockliss, Mrs.
Bromley and District Talking Newspaper Association.
Bromley and Beckenham Business and Professional Women's Club.
Bromley Borough Local History Society.
Bromley Council Education Department, staff of the building and sites division.
Bromley Council, Education Department, personnel section.
Bromley Camera Club.
Bromley High School (Junior School).
Bromley Junior Library, readers and staff.
Bromley Probus Club.
Bromley Road Infants' School.
Brookman, Mrs Doris.
Broughton, Mr and Mrs.
Brown, A.
Brown, Denise V. for her late brother Malcolm Brown and late sister Avril Brown.
Browne, Kathryn.
Browne, Michael.
Brown, Gwen of Brighton, South Australia.
Brown, Gwen Mrs.
Brown, H.J.
Brownies, 4th Penge.
Brownies, 5th Petts Wood West.
Brownies, 3rd Chelsfield.
Brown, Kathryn Mrs.
Brown, Miss J.D.
Brown, Mr and Mrs A.W.
Brown, Mr and Mrs C.T.
Brown, Mr and Mrs.
Brown, Mrs M.P.
Brown, Thomas Stephen.
Bruce, E.M.
Bruce, Margaret.
Bruce, Miss E.M.
Bryan, Mrs Aileen. In memory of her husband Arthur Bryan.
Bryan, Mrs Aileen.
Bryant, P.
Bull, E.
Bunting, Mrs W.M.
Burman, Mrs.
Burn, Mr and Mrs R.G.H. In memory of Helen Marsh.
Burnt Ash Infants School.
Burtonshaw, Miss B.E.
Butler, Mr and Mrs.
Butler, Wendy Ann.
Butler, Wendy.
Button, Mr and Mrs R.B.
Cabral, Leonora.
Caesar, Henrietta.
Calder, Margaret.
Campbell, Freda.
Campbell, Mr and Mrs K.J.
Campbell, J.M.
Campbell, Mr C.
Canter-Vischer, J and S.K.
Cant, Joseph. In memory of his wife, Doreen.
Carlin, Ian and Audrey.
Carrigan, Lily of Canada. On behalf of her late Aunt, Milly Dadswell and Uncle, Dadswell David.
Carr, Mr and Mrs John. In memory of Ted, Alice and Annie Carr.
Carr, Mr and Mrs John.
Carson, E.
Carter, Mr and Mrs J.H.
Carter, Mr and Mrs, and family.
Carter, R E.
Cartright, M.
Caton, Miss J.

Challenger, Mr and Mrs D.E.
Chamberlain, Mr and Mrs C.J.
Chandler, Ronald.
Chapman, Joan and Eileen Hayward.
Chapman, Mr and Mrs A.
Chapman, Miss Joan.
Chapman, Robin.
Chappell, Mr and Mrs A J.
Charles Darwin School, first year pupils.
Charles, Ms J E.
Charlton, Mr and Mrs E, and family.
Chase, Mr and Mrs A.M.
Chase, Nicholas.
Chase, Paul and Timothy.
Cheadle, Mr and Mrs L.D.
Chelsfield Village Society.
Cherry, Hannah.
Cheverton, Mr and Mrs J.
Chilman, Mr and Mrs A.G.
Chilton, Douglas.
Chilton, Joan.
Chilton, Mrs John.
Chislehurst Conservative Association's Thursday Club.
Chislehurst Methodist Badminton Club.
Chislehurst Methodist Church, youth club.
Choules, Mrs J.E.
Chuter, Mr and Mrs S.J. and the staff of Action Hire Centre of St Paul's Cray.
Clarke, Mrs A.M.
Clarke, Mr and Mrs K.T.J.
Clarke, Pat and Ron. In memory of Mrs Clarke's father and Mr Clarke's parents.
Clark, Liz.
Clark, Terry, Joyce, Christine, Simon and Vincent.
Cleaver, Miss P.W.
Clement, M.
Clenshaw, Mr and Mrs M.J.
Coles, Mr and Mrs N.
Coles, Pat and Peter.
Coles, Robin and Frances.
Coling, Mr and Mrs P.L.
Colins, Ian M.
Collens, J.A.
Collins, Mrs R.
Coltham, Mrs L.M.
Constantinides, Martin and Isabel Whitfield.
Conway, Lillian.
Cook, E and J.
Cook, Miss B M.
Cook, Mr and Mrs R. Gary and Andrew.
Cook, Mr and Mrs R.
Cook, Mr and Mrs E, in memory of CB
Cook, R.K.
Cook, R.W. and M.L.
Cooper, D.
Cooper, Mr and Mrs R.H.
Copers Cope Residents' Association.
Cornwell, Mr J.
Cornwell, I G.
Coughlan, Mr and Mrs B.
Coulson, A. And family.
Court, L.H.T. In memory of the late Marion Court.
Courtness, Misses C. and E. In memory of their parents.
Coward, Miss H.M.
Coward, Mrs F.M.
Cowden family of Chislehurst.
Cowing, Mr and Mrs E.G.
Cowing, Mr & Mrs I.
Cowling, W.
Coxwell, Jack.
Crabb, Mrs.
Craig, J.
Crampin, Ray and Audrey.
Cramp, Mr and Mrs J.A.
Cresswell, Mr and Mrs J.
Crofton Evening Townswomen's Guild.
Crofton Guide Company, 2nd.
Crofton Residents Association.
Croker, Mrs K.I.
Croker, William.

Cronin, Mr Pat.
Cropper, Ralph.
Crosby, Mrs F.V.
Cross, family.
Cross, Mr and Mrs Leslie.
Crowe G.
Crowe, Mr and Mrs E.D.
Crozier, Joan and Alison.
Cudham Village.
Cudham Village Club.
Cumbers, Miss M.E.
Cumbers, Mr W.E.
Cummings, Mr and Mrs.
Curd, Miss.
Cutbush, D.
Cuthbert Joan.
Dadswell, David and the late Milly.
Dalton, Eric, Constance and Joy.
Dalton, J.
Dalton, Mr and Mrs.
D'Angelo, Elizabeth.
Dare, Jill.
Darrall, Mr and Mrs K.
Darrick Wood Evening Townswomen's Guild.
Davie, Mr and Mrs S.
Davies, David.
Davies, Jean.
Davies, Miss J.M.
Davies, Mrs.
Davis, J A.
Davis, Jean. In memory of her mother Mrs A. Dadswell.
Davis, Mr and Mrs T. In memory of Tsar.
Davis, Mrs D.A.
Dawes, Mrs J.M.
Dawson, Sonya.
Day, Alan and Hilary.
Day, Alan and Hilary.
Dean, Dr and Mrs T.
Deering, W.M.
de Maid, Mr R E.
Denbigh, Deirdre.
Denham, Elizabeth. In memory of her son Jamie.
Dewick, Richard.
Dick Moreland's family.
Dicks, of Bromley.
Dilling, O.A. and H.J.
Dines, Mr and Mrs A.R.
Dines, Mr & Mrs.
Dining, H I.
Diston, Mr and Mrs A.R.
Dixon, Mr and Mrs R.
Dommett, Carol in memory of her mother, Annie Hinson.
Dorling, Richard.
Doughty, Paul, Dean and Colin and Avis Hyman.
Dove, Len and Florence.
Dover, R.H.W.
Downe May Queen Group.
Downing, K.
Drew, Eileen Leonora.
Drewett, Mr and Mrs Albert.
Drew, Mr and Mrs J.R.
Driscoll, Miss E.E.
Dryland, Mr and Mrs.
Duffin, Mr and Mrs G.
Dulake, Mr and Mrs.
Duncan, Mr and Mrs Dennis.
Dunne, E.C.
Dunworth, Mrs S.
Dyne, Mr and Mrs G.G.
Eales, J.
Eames, Mr and Mrs F.G.
Eames, Mrs K.M. In memory of her late uncle Bert Blundell, for many years verger at St Giles, Farnborough and her late father Frank Williams.
Eastick, Mr and Mrs L.E.K.
Eaton, Miss L.H.
Eden Park Residents Association, Beckenham.
Edgerton, Mr and Mrs B.L. in memory of Eric W Ridley.
Edgerton, Bertha L in memory of Eric W Ridley.

Edmands, Mr and Mrs Bickley.
Edmands, Mr and Mrs G.
Edmonds, Mrs.
Edwards, Cecil and Eve.
Edwards, Joan.
Edwards, Michael.
Edwards, Mr and Mrs H.J.
Edwards, Marion and Brian.
Edwards, M J.
Ekins, S.
Elder, Mr and Mrs Frank.
Eley, Beatrix.
Elmore, Mr and Mrs David.
Elphick, Misses.
Enviroment Bromley.
Evans, Mrs F.M.
Evans, Mrs J.F.
Fagg, Mr and Mrs R.
Fallows, Clare.
Fallows, Mrs C.E.
Farmelo, Mr and Mrs C.A.
Farnborough Friendship Club. In memory of 'Johnny' Johnson.
Farnborough District Guides and Brownies.
Farnborough Park Residents' Association.
Farnborough Friendship Club.
Farnborough (St Giles) Guide Company, 5th.
Farnborough Village Society.
Farnborough Dramatic Society.
Farnborough Women's Institute.
Fawcett, Somporn.
Feltham, Mr and Mrs J.W.
Fender, Beth.
Fenlon, Mr and Mrs Dennis.
Ferguson, Mr and Mrs.
Ferrar, V.
Fish, Eileen.
Fisher, Mrs G.
Fisher, Tony and Eve.
Fivaz, D.
Fletcher, Joy and Geoff.
Fletcher, Mr and Mrs D.A.
Flower, B.D.G.
Flower, Mr and Mrs Graham.
Flowers, H E.
Fogg, Mr.
Ford, Adele and Nicole.
Ford, A.D.
Ford, Mrs C in memory of her husband, William George.
Ford, W G.
Fowell, Miss L.
Fowler, Joyce and John.
Fowler, Mrs P.
Fox, Dianne and Steve.
Francis, Mr and Mrs R.
Franks, Mrs M.K.
Frank, W.
Fraser, David.
Freebairn, Mary.
Freeman, Mrs M.
Fry, Alan and Kathryn.
Fuller, Mr and Mrs C.
Gabroughton, Mr.
Gaigh, Mrs D.S.
Gammon, Mary, Geoff, Sara and Rachael.
Gardiner, Mrs M.
Garfield, Brian S.
Garner, Mrs H.
Garner, Mrs Joan.
Garwood, Mrs R.D.
Gates, Joan.
Gates, Miss W.M.
Gaylor, Joan.
Gaylor, Mrs J.M.
George, Mr and Mrs M.
Gerrish, L.P. and M.
Gibbons, Doreen.
Gibbs, Mr and Mrs S.W.
Gibson, Coral.
Gibson, J.W. and M.E.A.
Giffiths, Mr and Mrs G.F.

Gillard, Mrs P.
Glebe Housing Association.
Glendinning, Lilian.
Glover, Eileen. In memory of her late husband Ronald Bertram Glover.
Glynn, Mary and Stanley.
Godbee, Mrs G.
Goddard, Miss D.
Goddington Nursery, children of Green Street Green, Parish of Halliwell, Mr and Mrs F, of New Southwales, Australia.
Goemans, Geoffrey and Joan.
Goffin, S.
Goldsmith, Mr.
Goodchild, G.V.
Goodchild, Mrs M.
Goodhart, Sir Philip, MP for Beckenham and Lady Goodhart.
Gooding, Bernadette and Steve.
Goodwin, Marjorie. In memory of her late parents, Gwendoline and George Goodwin.
Goose, Rosemary Julia in memory of her husband Donald.
Gordon, A and L.
Gosling, Mrs F.
Govier, Mr and Mrs A.C.
Gower, Professor and Mrs D.B.
Graham, Frances.
Graham, Philip.
Grantham, Mr and Mrs E.M.
Grant, H.
Green, E.F.
Greenhaigh, Miss C M L.
Greenhalgh, Miss C.M.L.
Green, Mr and Mrs D.J. and Jeremy.
Green, Mr and Mrs D.
Green, Mr and Mrs E.
Green, Mr & Mrs E.
Green, Mrs J.
Green Street Green Cub Pack, 1st, and 1st Green Street Green Brownie Pack.
Green Street Green Venture Scout Ranger Guide Unit, 1st.
Gregory, Marjorie.
Griffin, Doris.
Griffins, Mr and Mrs G F.
Griffith, Mr and Mrs B.G.
Griffiths, C.J. and Y.P.
Griggs, Mr and Mrs C.
Grimble, R.F.B.
Grimshaw, A.
Grimshaw, Mrs E.
Grimwade, Miss E.
Grimwood, A.
Grossi, Mrs F.V.
Grubb, Esq.
Gugas, Mrs C.
Guide dog Meole.
Guides, 7th West Wickham.
Guinkey, Roberta.
Gunn, Mr and Mrs A.
Gunn, Nicola and Karen.
Guntrip, Mr and Mrs J.A.
Hadley, Mr and Mrs.
Hague, Jennifer.
Haigh, Doreen. In memory of her late husband A.M.Haigh.
Haime, Mrs J.H.
Haime, Mrs D.
Haines, I.
Halaby, Joyce.
Hale, Ann.
Hale, Mrs.
Hale, Nicholas, of Connecticut, U.S.A.
Hale, Sarah.
Haliwell, Mr and Mrs F.
Hall, Anne.
Halliwell, Mr and Mrs F.
Hall, Marion in memory of her parents, Charles and Nellie Hammond.
Hall, Mrs M.
Hall, Sheila Maureen.

Halstead, Margaret.
Hammett, B.J. and P.J.
Hammond, Miss L.F.
Hanchett, Mr and Mrs R.S.
Hanna, Jenny. In memory of her late parents, Violet and Percy Harwood.
Harbour, Mrs M.M.
Harding family.
Hardy, Mr. P.
Hardy, P.
Harman, Mary. In memory of her late father, Sidney Harman.
Harris, Mrs J.M.
Harrison, Mrs B.
Harrower, Mrs R.
Hart, Mr and Mrs G.C.
Hartree, Jacquey.
Harvey, J.W.
Harvey, Professor and Mrs L.P.
Hastings, Mrs R.
Hathorn, Mrs M in memory of George Edward Carter, Albert Carter and Horace Butler.
Hathorn, Mrs M.
Hatton-Jones, Ms Ann.
Hawkins, Esther and family. In memory of their late parents, Edwin and Elizabeth Louisa Hawkins.
Hayes branch, Royal British Legion Women's Section.
Hayes Flower Club.
Hayes (Kent) Village Association.
Hayes Trefoil Guild.
Hayhow, Sophie and David.
Haynes, M.A.
Hayward, Doris.
Hayward, R W.
Haywood, Mrs Eileen.
Hazelden, S.
Hazell, Miss.
Head, Douglas and Shirley.
Heaford, Tony, age 9.
Heath, Mr and Mrs S.W.
Hellicar, Christine, Chief Reporter Bromley Times.
Henden, Mrs A.
Henry, Gareth and Gavin.
Hickey, S.
Hickmer, Mr and Mrs H.
Hicks, E.
Hicks, Miss B.
Hicks, Mr and Mrs G.A.
High Elms Golf Club.
Higton, Mr and Mrs D.I.R.
Hillier family of Beckenham.
Hill, Mary.
Hill, Mrs.
Hill, S.M.
Hinton, D.
Hitchcock, D.J.
Hitchman, Mr and Mrs R.J.
Hoadley family.
Hobbs, A.S and W.E.
Hobbs, D.H.
Hobbs, H.J. and I.D.
Hobbs, Mr & Mrs M L.
Hobbs, Mrs D.
Hobbs, Mrs Pat.
Hodges, Mr and Mrs Anthony.
Hodgman, Beth aged 10, of Devon.
Hodson, Charles, Mary and John.
Hoearth, Ms Fiona.
Holdsworth, Mr and Mrs M.
Holland, Mr and Mrs R.
Hollingum, Mrs A.E. and Miss B Wishart, Mrs M.F. In memory of her father, Christopher James Wythe.
Holloway, Mrs Marion. In memory of her mother, Brenda Ledger and stepfather, Frederick Ledger.
Holmes, David. In memory of his friend Stanley Williams.
Holmes, David and Edna.
Holmes, Mr and Mrs David.
Holmes, M.
Holt, L.G.

Holt, Mary.
Holton, W.F. and M.E.
Hookey, Mrs and Miss.
Hopkins, Joan.
Hopkins, M.
Horler, Mrs P.
Howard, Ida.
Howell, Mr and Mrs R.F.
Hoy, D.
Hoy, Mr and Mrs P.H.
Hubbard, Mr and Mrs R.
Hubbard, P.
Hubert, Miss W.J.
Hudson, John.
Huggan, Betty.
Hughes, Margery.
Hulf, D.G.
Humphries, Mrs J.
Hunt, Mrs P.B.
Hurlock, Mrs R and family.
Hurst, C.
Hutchings, R.N.
Hyams, Derek and Elisabeth.
Inglis, H.D.
Ireland, S.
Irens, E.C.
Jacklin, Mr and Mrs J.
Jackson, Fred and Pamela.
Jackson, Joyce.
James, H.E and E.M.
James, Mr and Mrs A.T.
James, Mrs L.V.
James, Nicholas.
James, N.
Jarvis, C J.
Jarvis, John Boynton King.
Jarvis, Miss G.
Jayne, Una.
Jean Asherton
Jeffreys, S.
Jenkins, Rhian and Owen.
Jermyn, P.
Jessiman, Dr Ian.
Johnson, Mr R.L.
Johnson, Mrs D.
Johnson P.M.
Johnson, Peter.
Johnson, R.L.
Jolliffe, I.F. In memory of Lt. Col. J.J. Jolliffe, MBE, MC,MM.
Jones family of Petts Wood.
Jones, H and Z.
Jones, Reg and Iris.
Jones, Sarah.
Jones, Simon.
Jorgensen, Mr and Mrs John.
Jury, Mr and Mrs D.
Katchoff, Mr and Mrs B.S.
Kay, John.
Kay, Sybil.
Keates, Thomas and Joy.
Keegan, David and Joyce.
Keeley, Sue and Ron.
Keir, Margaret.
Kelsey, Miss N.P.
Kelsh, Mr and Mrs N.G.
Kemish, Joyce.
Kemp, Mr and Mrs.
Kennedy, Mrs J.
Kerner, Hilda, Valerie and Linda. In memory of Albert and Howard.
Kerr, A.W.
Keston Mark Residents' Association.
Kettel, John and Sheila.
Kidd, C.A.
King, K.C.
King, Miss.
Kingsbury, Mr and Mrs Herbert.
Knapp, Dee, Tony and family. In memory of Mum, Mrs Lilian Clarke.
Knight, G. In memory of Robert Knight.
Knight, Mrs M.L.

Knoll Residents' Association, Orpington.
Knowlden, Mr and Mrs W.G.
Knudsen, June and Lenore Smith of Toronto, Canada
Kormendy, Mr and Mrs L.P.
Kunsden, Miss J.
Laban, Mr T.
Laban, T.
Ladd, Susan.
Ladycroft Women's Institute (evening branch of Farnborough Village WI).
Lamborn, Miss J.S.
Lancaster-Smith family of Bickley.
Langley Park School for Boys, Beckenham.
Lang, Miss F.I.
Langridge, Mr and Mrs.
Lansbury, Edna.
Lansdell, Mr and Mrs D.
Last, Miss P A.
Last, Mrs.
Latuskie, Theresa.
Lavenal, J.
Lavender, Mr and Mrs L.
Laverick, J and J Craig.
Lawrence, Mr and Mrs M.J.
Layne, Mr & Mrs.
Layng, Mr and Mrs.
Leach, Mrs E.M.
Leadley, Mr and Mrs J.S.K.
Leary, Miss M.
Leaves Green Residents' Association.
Ledger, Albert D.
Ledger, Betty. In memory of her late husband, John.
Lee, G.R.
Lee, Mr and Mrs H.
Lee, Mrs S.
Lees, Mr and Mrs B.
Leeson's Primary School, St Paul's Cray.
Leggett, Colin and Hazel.
Leggett, Miss M.
Leigh, Mrs B.
Lettington, Betty.
Letton, Miss D.
Liddon, A.R. and F. In memory of Frank McCarthy.
Liffen, Mr and Mrs.
Lilly, M.D. and S.E.
Littlewood, Mrs N.
Livermore, Paul.
Livermore, Paul.
Lloyd, A and S B, in memory of E W Ridley.
Lloyd, Mr and Mrs.
Lloyd, Mrs E.M. and Miss Goddard.
Lloyd, Stephen, Barbara and Alex.
Locksbottom Cricket Club. In memory of Penny Walker.
Locksbottom Cricket Club.
Lockwood family.
Lomax, I.
London Borough of Bromley, Planning Department, Room N2.
London Electricity Board.
Longstaff, Mr and Mrs P.L.
Lord, Mr and Mrs E.H.
Lowe, D.
"Lucky".
Ludeman, Joe and Joan.
Ludeman, Jane.
Ludeman, Keith, Diane, Emma and Claire.
Lunn, Mr and Mrs R.M.
Lyddall, Mr and Mrs R.
Lynch, Mrs.
Lyon, Cliff and Brenda.
Lyon, Crista.
Lyon, Mrs Crista.
Mackay, Mr and Mrs A.D.
Mackay, Mr and Mrs.
Mackintosh, Annette.
Maid, de R.C.
Maier, Gill, Clive, Miles and Karen.
Major, Mrs B. In memory of her daughter, Mrs Ann Perris.
Mangat family.
Mann, Mrs R.

Marks, Mr and Mrs A.F.
Marshall, Mr and Mrs.
Marshall, M.J.
Marshall, Mrs.
Martinloat, Mrs D.
Martin, Miss M.
Martin, Mr & Mrs.
Marum, Mr and Mrs M.A.B.
Mascard, Mrs V.
Mason, W.
Masters, L.G.
Masters, Lenore.
Mathews, Mrs P in memory of her husband, Stuart.
Maxwell, Jean and David.
May, Colin, Gladys and John.
Mayhew, Mrs R.E.
Mazinke, Mrs S.
McAleer, Mrs.
McAllister, Betty.
McCarthy, Mrs G. In memory of her late husband Frank.
McCarthy, Mrs A.
McComb, Mrs J.H.
McCririck, Mr.
McGreghan, Ms Diana.
McHale, Ellie.
McHale, Thomas.
McInnes, Mr and Mrs D.
McLenehan, W.M.
McLetchie, Miss L.
McMillan, A.G.
McQuiggan, John.
Medhurst, Gwen and Joan Hopkins.
Medhurst, Mrs J.G.
Medhurst, Gwen.
Meehurh, Miss J.M.
Meredith, C.H. In memory of Winifred Elizabeth.
Meredith, Mr and Mrs W.G.
Merritt, Pauline.
Mervin, Mrs O, of Digby, Nova Scotia, Canada.
Michale, Ellie.
Michale, Thomas.
Michels, Mr and Mrs.
Miller, Cindy.
Mills, Miss A.E.S.
Mills, Mr and Mrs A.J.
Mills, Paul.
Milne, Sister, Bromley Hospital.
Milnes, Mrs J.
Mind, Miss D.
Miss Smith.
Mitchell, N.W.
Mobbs, Marguerite.
Molyneux, Mr and Mrs G.
Moneur, Lorna.
Moody, Andrew and Nicholas.
Moody, Pat and Alan.
Moores, D.
Moorhouse, Ms V A.
Moreland, Dick, from his family in his memory.
Morgan, D.H.
Morgan, Mrs M. in memory of her parents, G and L Price.
Morgan, Mrs M in memory of Eric W. Ridley.
Morgan, Mrs Marjorie.
Morgan, Raymond for Jessie McClean Morgan.
Morley, Mr and Mrs and Family.
Morris, Mr K.J and Mrs P.A. In memory of the late Mr J.H. and Mrs E.V.W.Morris.
Morris, Mr and Mrs.
Morrow, Mr and Mrs R.S.
Mortimer, K.V.
Mortimer, Joan Ethel.
Morton, Mr and Mrs Tony.
Moss, Mr and Mrs L.T.J.
Moss, Mr and Mrs T.
Moss, Olive.
Mowles, Mrs I.
Moxon, C.
Moyer, Emma.

Mr and Mrs Philip Graham for their son, Matthew David.
Mr & Mrs Smith.
Muir, Christina.
Murray, Colin Grant. In memory of his father, Alec Grant Murray.
Murray, Mr and Mrs E.
Murray, R.A.
Murray, Sarah Jane.
Murrie, Mrs M. In memory of her late husband.
Murrie, Mrs I F in memory of her husband.
Mutton, Miss E.M.
Nealon, M.
Negus, Rita.
Nemesis Baton Twirlers of Orpington.
Nevard, Mr and Mrs N.S.
Neville, Christopher.
Newcomb, Mr and Mrs D.H.
Newman, B.P. and J.B.
Newman, Eileen.
Newstead Wood School, Orpington.
Newth, Miss J.V.M.
Nicholson, Mrs E.
Nicholson, Mr and Mrs S.
Nickelson, Arthur.
Nightingale, Brian Charles, Caroline Elizabeth and Mark Richard
Norland, Mr and Mrs O.R.
Norman, J.O.
Norman, Mrs O.
Novi, Mrs C.
Nugent, Mr and Mrs D.L.
Nuthall, Mr and Mrs R.A. and family in memory of Alexander Armstrong and Edward Stacey.
Oakley, Cassie and Joe.
Oakley, Emma and Wonky.
Oakley, Lucy.
Oakley, the rest of the family.
Obee, June.
O'Connell, Mrs P.
Ogden, Mr and Mrs B.
Ogilvie, H.G.
Oldaker family of Horton Kirby.
Old Hill and Cudham Lane North Residents' Association.
Oliver, Edith.
Omerton Ltd, staff.
Oregon Park Residents Association.
Orford, Susan.
Orpington Branch of the Association of Men of Kent and Kentish Men.
Orpington College of Further Education, library staff.
Orpington Liberal Association.
Orpington Library, readers and staff.
Orpington Amateur Repertory Club, Junior section.
Orpington Horticultural Society.
Orpington Afternoon Group.
Orriss, Frances and Alfred.
Osborne, Michael.
Osborne, Miss E.
Oscroft, Jean.
O'Sullivan, A Jeanne.
Oxwell, Jack.
Packer, E.G.
Packham, David.
Padgham, Mrs P.
Page, Mr and Mrs J.
Paine, Kathleen, Lilian.
Paine, Mrs P. In memory of Reginald James and May Cottrell.
Palk, Nigel.
Palmart, Mrs G.
Palmer family of Beckenham.
Palmer, Mr.
Palmer, Mrs.
Pamment, Miss V.E.
Paris, G.H.
Parker, Neil, Claire and Hannah.
Park Langley Residents' Association.
Patrick, Mr and Mrs A.R.
Payne, Mrs E.B.

Pearce, Kathleen.
Pearce, Mrs T.H.
Pedley family of Orpington.
Peers, Mr and Mrs.
Pendred, D.
Penge Brownie Pack, 4th.
Pentelow, Miss G.
Peploe, Mr and Mrs G.C.
Pepper, Ann. To celebrate the golden wedding of Stanley and Evelyn Sims.
Pepper, Anne.
Pepper, Brenda in memory of her husband, John.
Pequignot, Clifford.
Perrett, John and Margaret.
Perry, Mr and Mrs W.
Peters, Mr and Mrs D.S.
Peterson, M.N.
Petts Wood Scout Group, 7th.
Petts Wood Floral Art Club.
Petts Wood Residents' Association.
Philips, K.
Philips, Mr and Mrs Roger, and family.
Philips, Rose.
Phillips, Audrey.
Phillips, Mrs R.
Pickhurst Mead Residents, Hayes.
Pike, J.
Pilcher, Leonard.
Pingstone, Gordon, chairman, Kelsey Park Estate and District Protection Association, Beckenham.
Pink, Barbara.
Pirt, Janet.
Pitt, Mr and Mrs R.
Platt, Miss H.G.
Plowman, Mr and Mrs R.E.
Pointon, Mrs M.
Pollard, Nigel and Patricia.
Poll, G.W.
Pomeroy, Mrs J O.
Pooley, Miss D.E.
Portsmouth, Mrs J.
Postlewaite, Doris.
Potter, Mrs B.
Poulter, D M.
Poverest Club Scout Pack, 1st.
Poverest Infants School, St Mary Cray.
Poverest Junior School, St Mary Cray.
Powell, Miss B.
Powell, Miss P.
Prescott, Mrs B and family.
Prime, Mrs M.
Princes Plain Primary School.
Pritchitt Foods, of Bromley.
Proctor, Mr and Mrs A.
Pryde family of Bromley. In memory of Frances Moss.
Pulfer, Mrs E.B.
Pulling, Mr and Mrs.
Queen Mary House, Chislehurst. The residents.
Quinton, Miss.
Rabbets, Miss I.A.
Raglan Infants School, Bromley.
Raikes, Mrs W.
Ramsden School for Boys, tutor and boys of form 5DW, A.E Oates, Richard Hemming, Simon Longhurst, Danny Morris, Paul Brett, Michael Berry, Michael Gard, Andrew Wallace, Barry De Souza, Justin Colenso, Eddie Ranger, Scott Baker, Martin Garrard, Nicholas Lane, Philip Ade, Anthony Allen, Stuart Turner, Lam Phan and Glen Rogers.
Randall, Dr and Mrs K.J.
Randall, Mrs K.J.
Rayfield, Peter and Barbara.
Rayfield family of Orpington.
Reading, Councillor Brian, of Beckenham.
Redfern, Mr and Mrs C.
Rediffusion Reditune Ltd.
Redmond, Richard.
Reed, Mr and Mrs Cyril.
Regan, Mr and Mrs N.A.
Rennie, W.D.
Rice, Miss P. In memory of her late father Thomas Rice.

Richards, Lynda and John.
Rickman, Mark.
Rickson, Derrick and Patricia.
Ridley, Mrs M in memory of her husband, Eric
Rigden, Mr and Mrs D.G.
Righini, Mavis.
Roberts, Dr M.E.
Robertson, Mr and Mrs J.C.
Robertson, Mrs E.
Robertson, Neil and Timothy.
Robinson, Margaret.
Robson, Mr and Mrs N.C.
Rockall, Tom and Rose.
Roe, Mrs J.
Roff, Enid.
Rogers, A.
Rogers, Pauline M.
Rogers, Trevor and Vanessa.
Ronalds, Mrs E.J.
Rose, Russell.
Ross, Enid.
Rossier, Philip.
Ross, Mrs D.M.
Ross, Mrs Enid H.
Roth, Mr and Mrs L.G.
Rowland, Mr and Mrs G.A.
Royce, Mr.
Rudd, Mrs R.
Rush, Eric.
Russbridge, Miss.
Russell, Michael and Joyce.
Russell, Mr and Mrs.
Ryan, Mr and Mrs S.F.
Sachs, Mrs N.M.
Saidi, Mr.
Saint, the family Cook, E and J. In memory of C.B. Grubb.
Salamon, Mrs P.H.
Sammut, Anthony.
Samuels, Mrs J.E.
Sansom, Miss H.
Sargent, Mr and Mrs Graham.
Savage, Michael and Shirley.
Saxby, R.
Saxton, Mrs E.G.
Sayer, Mr and Mrs E in memory of their son, Russell.
Scarborough, Mrs M.
Schenck, Margaret, Fiona and Melissa in memory of Eric W Ridley.
School Mistresses and Governesses Benevolent Institution
Schweizer, F. and J.
Scott, C.E. and D.M.
Scott, Diana.
Scott, Dr and Mrs G.W.
Scott, Dtment, Room N2, London Borough Of Bromley Williamson, Patricia and David.
Scott, Mr and Mrs L.A.
Scott, Mr and Mrs A.
Scott, Mrs C.E.
Scudamore, Mr and Mrs P.
Scuffham, A.
Scullard, Mr and Mrs P.A.
Seal, Ronald.
Seamer, A.R.
Sears, Linda.
Sea Venture Corps, TS Mary-Rose, Penge Unit.
Segal, A.
Sell, Mr and Mrs D.R.
Sellwood, Lynn and Philip.
Selsdon and Addington Cub Pack, 2nd, especially Red Six.
Sexton, Mrs.
Sharpe, S.T.
Shaw, Ellen.
Shawyer, Mr and Mrs.
Shears, Kenneth James.
Shelton, Jean and Jim.
Shepherd, E.
Sherborne, Frank.
Sherriff, Elizabeth, Carl and Kate.
Shill, Joy.

Shipton, M.
Siddall, Mrs P.
Simkin, Valerie.
Simmonds, Florence and William, of Pluckley.
Simmons, Mr and Mrs B.D.
Simpson, Gladys. In memory of her husband Henry Simpson.
Simpson, J.A and C.M.
Simpson, Mr and Mrs K.J.
Simpson, Neil.
Sims, Edward and Ann
Sinclair, Joan.
Slack, Mr & Mrs J R.
Slaughter, H.E.
Sloan, Mr and Mrs D.
Slow, E.N.
Small, Leonard and Marjorie.
Smith, Cannon A.E.
Smith, C R.
Smith, Edith and Grace.
Smith, Frances.
Smith, Lauren and James.
Smith, M and P.
Smith, Margaret and Peter.
Smith, Miss Hilda.
Smith, Miss D.E.
Smith, Miss Lauren and Master James Thomas.
Smith, Mr and Mrs E.C. On behalf of Patricia and David Williamson.
Smith, Mr and Mrs E.
Smith, Mr and Mrs A.
Smith, Mrs E.
Smith, Mrs L.
Smith, Ms Helen.
Smith, Richard David.
Smith, Rosemary. In memory of her parents Edmund Leslie Palmer and Mrs Veronica Palmer.
Social Democratic Party, Orpington constituency.
Sokoloff, Paul.
Somers, Dorothy.
Sones, Mrs J.
Sorrell, L.
Speight, Mr and Mrs.
Spence, P.M.
Spong, Mrs M.
Springett, Mr and Mrs H.M.
Stanley, Philip.
Steel, Mrs M.E.
Steer, Mr and Mrs J.A.C.
Stevens Mrs G E in memory of her husband Mr W A Stevens and her daughter Mrs A M Adams.
Stevens, Mr W.A. and Adams, Mrs A.M.
Stevens, Mrs G.
Stiles, J.R.
Still, Mr and Mrs R.K. In memory of their parents Mr and Mrs W. Still and Mr and Mrs P·G. Hickman.
Stillwell, Mr.
St Joseph's Primary School, Bromley.
St Luke's Ladies Guild, Bromley Common.
St Mary Cray Action Group.
St Mary's Ladies Group of Green Street Green.
St Mary's Parish Church, Green Street Green.
St Nicholas Friendship Club, Orpington.
Stobbs, D.
Stoneham, Miss B.
Stone, Mr and Mrs R.K.
Stone, Mrs E L.
Stone Richard and Debbie.
Streek, Angela and Jennifer.
Stuart, Arthur.
Sturgeon, Mr and Mrs E.R.
Sullivan, Eileen.
Summer, Mrs M.H.
Sundridge Residents' Association.
Swinyard, Mr and Mrs E.
Sydenham Society.
Tait, Miss Beryl.
Tapper, Yvonne and Robin, Orpington.
Taylor, Mrs Margaret. In memory of her father William Menzies.

Teasdale, Mrs.
Technical Services Department, Room M2, London Borough of Bromley.
Terry, Mr and Mrs M F, Patricia and Julie, in memory of Lucky and Mrs Roberta Grimley.
Terry, Mr and Mrs Michael.
Terry, Patricia and Julie.
Thomas, Marion.
Thompson family. In memory of Grace Partridge.
Thompson, A.A.
Thompson, Joe and Ben.
Thompson, Mr.
Thomson, Jessie.
Thomson, Linda and Pat Cronin.
Thomson, Mr & Mrs J D.
Thorn, J.C.
Thornton, T.P. and M.
Tilley, Mr and Mrs.
Tilly, Mrs C.
Tilly, N.
Tims, Mr and Mrs N.P.
Tindle, Mr and Mrs N.
Tintagel Ladies Club.
Tipton, Dennis and Margaret.
Titheridge, Mrs.
Titshall, Mr and Mrs A. and Miss N.
Todman, I.D.
Tombs, Anthony.
Tongue, Simon.
Tooher, Mr.
Towersey, Eunice. In memory of her parents, Frank and Bertha Towersey.
Tracy, Mrs P.
Treadle, Mr and Mrs N.M.
Treliving, Mr and Mrs N.E.
Trotman, Mavis C.
Turner, Christopher.
Turner, Irene and Geoffrey.
Turner, Mr D.S.
Turner, Penelope.
Tweedle, Mrs N.M. and Mr R.
Tyers, Miss I.
Tyrell, Mrs V.
Ustianowski, Dr and Mrs P.A.
Valenza family of Bromley.
Vallat, Mrs M.
Valley Primary School.
Venner, David.
Vidler, Mr and Mrs.
Villatt, Mrs H.
Vincent, Pete.
Vine, J.G.
Wade, Margaret. In memory of her parents Ruby and Baden Holder.
Wadsworth, Jennifer and Michael.
Walker, Albert, the family of in memory.
Walker, Florence. In memory of her parents, Montague and Florence Walker.
Walker, Louise.
Waller, Daniel and Claire.
Waller, Mr and Mrs J.L.W.
Wall, G.A.
Walter, Mr and Mrs D.
Ward, David and Barbara.
Wardhaugh, Steve.
Warner, G.W.C.
Warren, Mr and Mrs D.E.
Waterfield, Mr & Mrs.
Waters, Mr and Mrs G.E.
Wates Built Homes Ltd.
Watler Mr & Mrs D and S.
Watson, James.
Watson, Mr and Mrs C.
Watson, Mr and Mrs A.L.
Watson, Stephen and Philip.
Wayfarer Elfins Group of the Woodcraft Folk, based at Cudham.
Webb, Mrs R.
Webb, Pamela.
Welch, Dennis, Linda, Tracy and Terina.
Wells, A.G.
Wells, Mr and Mrs D.V.

Werrey-Easterbrook, Elizabeth.
West Beckenham Residents' Association.
West, Dr Michael and Mrs Lois.
West Mrs J.
West Wickham and Beckenham South Scout District.
West Wickham (South) Residents' Association.
West Wickham Residents' Association.
Whale, Patricia, Michael, Christopher, Stephen and the late John Whale.
Whatmough, Pamela, David, Matthew and Daniel.
Wheddon, George and Eleanor.
Wheeler, E.J.
Wheeler, Mr and Mrs G.
White, Edith. In memory of her late husband, Herbert John White.
White, Esme.
White, family.
White, Marion.
White, Mr and Mrs D.
White, Robert.
Whitfield, Isobel.
Whitlock, Mr and Mrs J.
Wild, E.N.
Wilkinson, Mrs L.M.
Wilkinson family.
Wilkins, Ray and Doreen.
Williams, Nigel.
Williams, D.
Williams, S.F. and G.J.
Williamson, P.
Williams, Mr and Mrs K.A.
Willis family.
Willis, H.W.
Willis, Mr and Mrs A.E.
Willmott, June.
Willsher, Mrs D.E.
Wilmot, V.
Wilson, Joan.
Wilson, Mr.
Winter, Mrs E.K.
Wishart, Mrs M F.
Wolstencroft, F.
Woodall, Mrs B.A.
Wood, Colonel B.R.
Wood, Daphne.
Woodhatch, Mrs J.
Woodman, Miss M N.
Wood, Mr and Mrs A.
Wood, Mrs M and Woodland Melissa.
Wood, Rev and Mrs Harold.
Woods, Mr and Mrs G.R.J.
Woods, Mr and Mrs Len.
Woods, Mr K.O.
Wooldridge, G.
Wooldridge, C.
Wooldridge, M.J.
Wooldridge, E.C.
Wooldridge, N.
Wooldridge, Mrs.
Woolgar, A.R.
Woollett, R.G. and M.C.
Woosnam, family.
Worth, Dan and Mike.
Wray, Ernest, Marion, Adam and Gavin.
Wren, Margaret.
Wright, George, Joan and Alan.
Wright, Roger and Ellen.
Yates, Pamela.
York, E.
York, K.
Zajic S.
Zissell, Mr and Mrs.
Zissell, M.J. and B.K.